GHOSTS OF
BOBBY
MACKEY'S
MUSIC WORLD

To Hannah,

Happy Hauntings!

[signature]

GHOSTS OF BOBBY MACKEY'S MUSIC WORLD

DAN SMITH

Haunted America

Published by Haunted America
A Division of The History Press
Charleston, SC 29403
www.historypress.net

First published 2013

Manufactured in the United States

ISBN 978.1.62619.222.5

Library of Congress CIP data applied for.

This book is dedicated to those who have experienced paranormal encounters so frightening, so completely overwhelming to the senses, that there is no doubt in their minds that the existence of the spirit world is true.

For those who have been ridiculed or outcast for sharing their terrifying stories with the world, rest assured that there are others out there who fully understand and appreciate the weight that a paranormal matter can place upon your shoulders. There are others like you who go through life with a new perspective about what is real and what is important.

This book, although dark, reminds me that life after death is most certainly real, and I will one day be reunited with those who I have lost during this journey we call life.

This book is also dedicated to the late Carl Lawson, who endured unimaginable horror yet was strong enough to tell the world his story.

CONTENTS

Acknowledgements   9

Preface   11

Introduction: The Most Haunted Nightclub in America   15

The Scope of the Haunting Explained   17

I. GENESIS

1. Origins   25
2. Scandal   31
3. Downfall   39
4. Family   47
5. Unrestricted   56

II. DIABOLICAL

6. Acquisition   71
7. Johana   76
8. Dominion   87
9. Imitation   92

III. AFTERMATH

10. Pursued   99
11. Crooked   105
12. Deception   111
13. Malignant   116
14. Possibility   125
15. Revelations   131

Bibliography   135

About the Author   141

ACKNOWLEDGEMENTS

This book is the work of a great many individuals. This project has been the toughest but most rewarding literary experience I have ever undertaken. Thank you to my dear friends who share the same paranormal passion that I do. You show support for a form of legitimate study that is often met with ridicule and disparaging comments. Your encouragement gives me hope for the future studies of paranormal phenomena.

Special thanks to Becca Wilson, whose help and support continually drove me forward toward the finish line. Without your help, compiling historical data alone would have been a monstrous undertaking. Your assistance was priceless when I was faced with a mountain of information to sift through.

To my daughters, Nevaeh and Fallon, thank you for inspiring me every day. I share this book with the hopes that your generation will have a much more complete understanding of the paranormal world.

Thank you to those who were willing to share their experiences with the world in the hopes that others will gain a healthy respect for just how real and life changing paranormal encounters can be.

Thank you to the many people, places, museums, libraries and historical societies that helped discover important historical information. Uncovering these many untold stories has created a clearer picture regarding a location steeped in mystery.

PREFACE

During the summer of 1995, I lived in Ferndale, Michigan, a suburb of Detroit. Strange things started happening around me that no one had an explanation for. Lights would suddenly turn on by themselves. Water faucets would unexpectedly come on in other rooms. By this time in my life, my parents had divorced, and I essentially had two homes. When these strange things began happening, I began to notice that they seemed to happen around me, no matter which house I was at.

Nothing seemed too frightening, but the odd happenings began to occur more frequently over the summer. I would watch as streetlights burned out when the car I was riding in drove underneath them. Not just one here and there. No, there were many streetlights that were rendered inoperable simply from my passing by. Lights and water faucets began to turn on by themselves. I was given lectures about the cost of energy and advised to turn off these things when I left a room.

As the weird events continued, my father took notice and didn't like what was happening. "Are you channeling?" he would ask me. The answer was no. I had no idea what was causing the bizarre and increasingly regular events. My father believed me to be involved in some sort of black magic or other unhealthy practices. While this was not the case, as time went on and things kept occurring, I began to have a precognitive feeling about them. I began to "know" when something would occur. To this day, I can't fully explain what the feeling was like. It was unlike any other sense I've ever experienced. Perhaps it was a sixth sense, but if it was, I had no control over it.

One evening, I was suddenly engulfed in this "feeling" and immediately alerted my father. Not an entire minute later, the television began changing channels while we looked frantically back and forth between the television and the remote control, which sat quietly on the coffee table in front of us. No sooner did the shock set in than we began hearing sporadic pounding sounds on the interior walls of the house. And then all at once, our eyes turned to an old chair sitting empty only a few feet away from us. What I saw that night changed my life forever.

The aged recliner was a hideous orange color that beckoned thoughts of pale pastels worn during the 1970s. Over time, the footrest became progressively difficult to open. One had to sit in the chair and physically pull as hard as possible on the lever in order to open the footrest. But as my father stood in the living room and I sat on the couch, we both watched as this empty recliner began to violently open the footrest and slam it closed. Not before and not since have I seen my father's face lose so much color so quickly. We were stunned. We bounded out the front door and gathered outside, not really sure of what had just occurred. We were visibly shaken, having no idea what the cause could be for what we just witnessed.

After that terrifying incident, the strange things became more and more infrequent and eventually stopped altogether. Following the incident, my father reported that he had to replace the paneling above his fireplace. He said that "demonic faces" began appearing in the grain, more and more each day. His wife beseeched him to have it removed from the home because it frightened her. The episode for me had a life-altering effect. I grew curious of what exactly had happened and began delving into the world of paranormal investigation and research.

Looking back with the knowledge I have today, it seems quite clear that what I experienced was a poltergeist haunting. The popular belief in today's paranormal research community is that a poltergeist haunting doesn't involve any actual ghosts at all. It is widely believed that poltergeist events are caused by a human agent who unknowingly affects his or her surroundings through what is known as psychokinesis. In essence, a person is haunting himself or herself without knowing it. This type of phenomena usually occurs during big life changes, such as divorce, women going through menopause or in adolescents, such as myself.

For years, I sought to find locations with alleged paranormal activity and would seek to make contact with the spirit world, longing to find out definitively if life after death existed. Since that incident, I've been working to learn more about and educate others on the inner workings of the paranormal world.

Technology has come a long way for us paranormal enthusiasts since the days of analog voice recorders and using baby powder to capture ghostly footprints. For fourteen years, I spent my spare time in abandoned buildings, gathering evidence of paranormal occurrences.

After moving to Cincinnati in 2008, I became enthralled with the rich history of the city. Combining my love of history and the paranormal, I developed a local ghost tour covering the many haunts in and around the Queen City. In 2009, I became somewhat disinterested in *only* gathering evidence of my encounters and wanted more. From all my experiences and encounters over the years, I now knew for sure that something strange was going on. I changed my focus to the question *what now?* I saw many routine things happening that seemed to suggest that there might be certain scientific laws governing the manifestation of ghosts. I wanted to push forward the study of the correlation between science and the paranormal world. Next, I founded a paranormal organization centering around the "what now?" aspect. Today, we strive to extrapolate data from our ghostly experiences and make sense of what is happening in order to continually push forward our research.

While developing the ghost tour in 2008, I began visiting the infamous country music bar on Licking Pike. From my first visit, something about the place captivated me. As it would turn out, the stories being told about the place were not just embellishments. I became shockingly aware of the dark side of paranormal research. In all my years of paranormal work prior to visiting Bobby Mackey's, I never encountered anything quite so inherently evil. I had heard the stories of caretaker Carl Lawson falling under a demonic possession, but I wasn't sure that I believed in nonhuman spirits.

Having now spent more than three hundred hours investigating the property when it is closed for business, I can say with certainty that there is something going on there beyond the scope of a regular haunt by human ghosts. The spirit voices that are captured know personal things about the people who visit, and many people report being followed home by the ghosts. The paranormal occurrences and spirit attachments I have seen and experienced firsthand are far out of proportion to a "normal" haunting by a human spirit.

During our adventure through the documented history and stories of paranormal encounters, we will be diving deep into the dark side and the real dangers of investigating the paranormal world. As a reader, some stories might seem unbelievable or impossible. I'm here to tell you that not only are these encounters possible, but they have actually happened. I myself have experienced numerous firsthand incidents over the years. We will explore this extreme paranormal hotbed and cover the complete factual history of the site, along with many stories of otherworldly confrontations, in order to give you the best understanding of exactly why these phenomena might be occurring today.

The Most Haunted Nightclub in America

H umanity has been asking the great questions of life for millennia. One of those questions is "What happens to us after we die?" Historically, this question has been left to psychics and mediums. These mediums would claim to conjure and speak with the dead in parlors with shocking regularity. In the early twentieth century, however, many so-called mediums were found to be deceiving their customers outright. Harry Houdini made it his life's passion to expose imposters preying on innocent people looking for answers. The imposters, however, were brought about by a period of enlightenment in this nation in which many people came to believe in the afterlife and ghosts.

Modern-day Americans are even more receptive to the idea that life after death is real. As the popularity of paranormal television programs has exploded, so too have the amount of people who use their time to go out and visit supposedly haunted locations to decide for themselves what is real. After hundreds of investigations when the club is closed for business, the enduring consensus in the paranormal community is that Bobby Mackey's Music World is one of the most haunted locations on planet Earth. The strange happenings have been chronicled by thousands of people who have stood within its walls.

Just minutes from downtown Cincinnati, the building sits positioned on the banks of the Licking River in Wilder, Kentucky. At first glance when driving past during the week, the building looks to have been forgotten by time and completely empty. Locals share legendary ghost stories from the unbelievable to the extremely horrifying. The truth behind the building and its haunted history is stranger and more frightening than fiction.

Introduction

Having been featured on numerous television programs, Bobby Mackey's Music World is visited by thousands of paranormal enthusiasts annually. Through the ghost stories told over the years, much of the truly startling history of this site has been lost to the ghost story of the week. But this lost history is exactly what provides the backdrop necessary for understanding the extreme paranormal claims of today.

Revered by some and purposely avoided by others, this façade stands as a dark and tragic reminder of what time can do to hearts, the toll it can take on lives and how souls can be forever intertwined with a horrible past. If the walls of this place could speak, they would likely tell terrible stories of lies, deception, murder, greed and death.

The unspeakable events that took place under the cover of these walls still resonate today. Just walking into the same room where gangsters gambled and made life-changing decisions is enough to give some people the creeps. The rooms where mafia henchman did the dirtiest of their deeds and where lives were abruptly ended still hold feelings of grief and sorrow today. Through each and every incarnation, this site has had a dubious past overflowing with misdeeds and misfortunes. The sins perpetrated here in the past are not well forgiven by time. Evidence of these dark days still lies scattered around the club and basement, from stage decorations to old menus showcasing "Fresh Maine Lobster Salad" for seventy-five cents.

When visiting the modern-day club, one does not require psychic abilities to sense the tragedy spilled in the environment. The long-lost days of gambling and murder are not so long lost with visual reminders such as a giant safe, leftover gambling chips and old signs boasting floor shows until 4:00 a.m. As we examine the history of the site and the unimaginable horrors that took place there, we will uncover numerous stories of encounters with unseen forces and learn exactly what drives people to explore this darkest of haunts.

Winding through implausible stories of terror, we will follow a caretaker who tells of outrageous encounters. His experiences were frighteningly real and would forever change his life. Many people continue to experience the strangest of paranormal phenomena around the club and will share their shocking stories with the world. We will also explore the strange science that lies beneath the club. Through the years of notoriety, the site has fallen victim to historical facts being distorted, exaggerated and misinterpreted. After spending an extreme amount of time researching and comparing fact to myth, this title will finally set the historical record straight so you may better understand the true foundations behind the paranormal episodes occurring at the site. Many facts contained herein are being told for the first time. Through putting together clues, we will unfold the story of the "Most Haunted Nightclub in America."

THE SCOPE OF THE
HAUNTING EXPLAINED

B obby Mackey's Music World is widely regarded as one of the most haunted locations not only in the United States but also in the entire world. The intense level of paranormal occurrences at the club rises high above the scope of a regular haunting. Historical facts and scientific explanation will be covered in addition to the paranormal claims to create a true sense of exactly why the building is home to some of the most startling paranormal episodes ever recorded.

In addition to these contributing factors, many paranormal terms will be used to give you a better understanding of the exact type of manifestations that occur around the property. The following guide will aid in an enhanced understanding of the wide variety of paranormal events that have been reported.

GHOSTS

For thousands of years, people have reported coming in contact with ghostly beings. Those searching for answers continually find that ghostly manifestations don't fit exactly within the laws of physics. The truth, however, is that these manifestations don't fit within *three-dimensional* physical laws.

With recent advancements in science, many new theories are taking shape. Among the most popular with paranormal enthusiasts are those under the umbrella of quantum physics, such as quantum mechanics (the quantum study of electromagnetic waves), quantum electrodynamics (the quantum study of electromagnetism) and quantum geometrodynamics (the quantum study of gravity, including string theory).

Within the new theories of quantum science, the existence of ghosts has not only become possible but also highly probable. Explaining quantum science isn't an easy thing to do. For the sake of generalizing the science and breaking down the core principle, quantum physics studies the science of possibilities. The laws that govern the quantum world are profoundly baffling and bizarre, such as particles being present in more than one location at the same time and the presence of an undetected form of matter called dark matter, to name a few. Many scientists have found a basis for explaining paranormal phenomena in their research; however, very few share their opinions publicly for fear of ridicule, losing funding or being outcast within their fields.

Classically, a ghost refers to the energy left in existence when a person's physical body dies, such as a disembodied spirit or soul. Although this energy is no longer associated with a physical body, it can still interact with and be perceived by the living.

Many researchers refer to the first Law of Thermodynamics, which is the Law of Conservation of Energy to rationalize the shift from a physical being to existing in a nonphysical or semi-physical state. The law states that the total amount of energy in an isolated system remains constant over time. The energy can change its location and form within the system, but it cannot be destroyed. An everyday example would be boiling water in a pan. As the water heats up, a phase change occurs and the state of the water changes from liquid into gas. Some researchers believe the same is true for humans who experience death of the physical body; a phase change occurs, and the energy still exists in a different form.

Evidence to support a "soul" is strong, as we will explore. Those who encounter ghosts are interacting with the same essence that was present during life in the physical body. Ghosts seem to have the same habits, biases and general personality that they represented when they were living humans. This topic brings with it great debate in the area of paranormal studies. Some believe that this proves the existence of a soul, while others believe it is only energy left behind that has somehow been imprinted into the fabric of space-time.

Whatever the case might be, reports of encounters with ghosts continue to occur around the world. In a 2013 survey, the *Huffington Post* reported that 45 percent of Americans believe in ghosts or that the spirits of dead people can come back in certain places and situations.

TYPES OF PARANORMAL PHENOMENA

Many phenomena are associated with the existence of ghosts. The following are the types that will be explored in this book.

Apparition

An apparition is a manifestation that can be visually perceived as resembling a physical form. These manifestations can include human forms as well as animals. When seen, an apparition is identifiable by the viewer with recognizable features. They might appear as an entire body or in the form of a partial manifestation, in which only certain features are visible, such as arms or legs. Apparitions can occur as a result of a residual haunting or an intelligent haunting.

Shadow Figures

These dark masses are known as having a humanoid shape. The forms have no identifiable features, only the black outline of a figure. It is currently unclear whether shadow figures represent a residual manifestation, an intelligent haunting or both.

Electronic Voice Phenomena (EVP)

These voices occur on magnetic recording devices but are not heard by human ears at the time they occur. Many—though not all—EVP occur in a frequency range lower than the human ear can perceive, which is why the sound is not heard by humans at the time of capture. Some voices are direct answers to questions, while others are totally out of context, as if a third-party conversation has been captured. Because spirits do not have physical bodies or vocal cords to move wind through, how these voices are created remains unknown.

Voice Phenomena (VP)

These spirit voices are actually heard by human ears in the environment as they occur. Many researchers refer to EVP and VP as "disembodied voices." Voice phenomena is usually described as close enough in physical locality to be heard but sounding like it's coming from a far distance away.

Intelligent Spirits

This form of haunting is most closely associated with the classical understanding of the term "ghost." These spirits of deceased humans can have intelligent interactions with the living. They seem to continue to exhibit the same essence they had while they were alive, such as personality, emotions, habits, biases, smells and clothing. They are aware of what is happening in the present and can react to changes in the environment, such as renovations of a home or business. Some intelligent spirits are benevolent, considerate and friendly, while others are malevolent, angry and vengeful.

Inhuman Spirits

This title indicates spirits who have never had a human incarnation. They include animals, angels and what many religions refer to as "demons." Within the context of this book, the inhuman spirits are demonic in nature and seek the destruction of human life. These demonic entities strive to wreak havoc on the living. They have the ability to appear in the form of a human spirit. It is said, however, that when they manifest this way, there is always a distorted portion of the form. According to clergy, they are unable to fully impersonate a human perfectly because they have never had a human incarnation. They will use deeply personal information against you and are known to mimic familiar voices or appear as innocent apparitions such as children in order to deceive the living. It is believed that inhuman spirits are not restricted by space or time and possess much more incredible physical capabilities than human spirits.

Demonic Possession

This term refers to an inhuman entity taking control of a human's emotions, thought, intellect and personality by merging with his or her consciousness. The human then loses the ability, either partially or fully, to control his or her actions. The inhuman entity will then use this control to harm the person possessed or others. A possessed person does not usually know he or she is possessed until the late stages occur and others notice his or her outward changes.

Poltergeist

Coming from the German word meaning "noisy ghost," a poltergeist is known as an extremely dangerous and damaging manifestation. Objects might move of their own volition, very loud noises can be created and physical interaction with the living can occur. In some extreme cases, people themselves can be levitated or thrown by this unseen force. A poltergeist haunting has classically been considered to be an especially mischievous ghost wreaking havoc on the living. In the modern-day world of paranormal studies, however, many researchers believe that a poltergeist might not involve a ghost at all. The belief is that intense amounts of psychokinetic energy are unleashed by a human "agent," which causes a person to manifest seemingly paranormal occurrences. These include electrical disturbances, moving objects, water turning on or off or toilets flushing. Poltergeist activity seems to center around people who are going through tumultuous times in their lives, such as adolescents, pregnant women, those experiencing an exceptionally emotional death or women going through menopause. The disturbances seem to follow the agent to different locations, yet many times the person causing the phenomena has no idea they are responsible.

Residue Haunting

Also known as a *residual haunting* or *imprint*, this type of paranormal phenomenon occurs when an event is imprinted into the earth's environment. When this occurs, the event can play back in the environment like a recording. This type of manifestation may include sounds, smells, disembodied voices or apparitions. The key to understanding a residue haunting is that there is no intelligence behind the episodes. As the name suggests, only the residual effects of an event are left behind. Researchers do not fully understand the recording capability that the earth holds. It is believed these events have been imprinted onto the environment similar to the way information is imprinted onto DVDs, CDs or other media.

PART I

GENESIS

CHAPTER 1

ORIGINS

A strange and unfamiliar sound slowly leaked through the walls of a quiet bedroom. As the commotion continued, a man gradually opened his eyes and went into a full stretch across his bed. With his arms and legs shaking while stretching, he opened his eyes wider and became aware of his surroundings. As he lay there, alone in the darkness, a perplexed look came over his face. The sound of music continued to pour over him as he slowly sat up in the bed.

He stood up from the bed and walked calmly down a set of stairs, coming closer to the source of the sound. The wooden steps creaked beneath his feet as he stepped off the staircase and rounded the corner. As he approached the sound, it became increasingly clamorous and filled the entire room. Looking around, the man witnessed the nightclub that he lived above. The space, however, was indeed different than he had left it before retiring to bed. Lights that were turned off now illuminated the bar and stage. Standing in front of the source of the sound, the man stared in disbelief at what his eyes were seeing. A jukebox inside the nightclub was proudly and emphatically playing an old-fashioned tune through its speakers, filling the club with the sounds of days gone by. The man listened as the tune belted out words of love and desire. The song playing was the "Anniversary Waltz."

Pressing buttons in a panicked attempt to stop the music, he quickly gave up and unplugged the machine. The man gazed around with an intense look on his face, swiftly turning his eyes from one direction to another.

He fully expected to find some unauthorized person lurking in the club. Instead, he found only an empty space filled with an eerie silence. Stopping in his tracks, his eyes looked back and forth while his head was unmoved. Suddenly his voice rose from the silence. "Leave me alone!" he screamed. He then moved toward the light switches, turned them off once again and hastily returned back up the stairs to his apartment. He threw himself on his bed in disgust, feeling both inconvenienced and panic-stricken. Lurking in the shadows was a force so strong and so evil that it would soon take hold of the man's life entirely. The man was Carl Lawson, and he had no idea that the long list of events he was experiencing would take their toll on him and forever change the way he viewed the world. Soon, he would be completely consumed by the evil force and would endure the most terrifying experience of his life when he fell under a demonic possession.

FIRST VIEWS

On July 9, 1755, a group of British soldiers were engaged by a party of French and Indians near modern-day Pittsburgh. Although outnumbered roughly four-to-one, the French and Indians struck with such force and surprise that nearly all of the British were killed. It would become known as Braddock's Defeat. In a letter home, a twenty-three-year-old man told his mother of the slaughter in his own words. He wrote, "I was the only person left to distribute the General's orders, which I was scarcely able to do as I was not half recovered from a violent illness that had confined me to my bed and wagon for above ten days." The letter came from George Washington, who would later become president of the United States. The defeat was devastating and left the survivors suffering horrific nightmares of the slaughter that occurred. Among the few survivors at Washington's side was Colonel James Taylor.

In the fall of 1779, the land office in Virginia opened for the sale of land warrants. Colonel James Taylor acquired 5,333⅓ acres in Virginia. His son, General James Taylor Jr., would become responsible for clearing the land and laying out roads. A portion of this land was in Virginia on the banks of what would become known as the Licking River. It wouldn't become known as Kentucky until 1792.

The Taylors were a prominent family of Virginia, having been related to both former president James Madison and Zachary Taylor, who would go on to become president. On April 1, 1792, twenty-two-year-old James Taylor Jr. set out from his father's plantation with three slaves. They were headed to the newly formed state of Kentucky and wouldn't reach the area known as Newport until June 20.

When arriving, the group stayed at Fort Washington in Cincinnati. During that summer, the three slaves, Humphrey, Adam and Moses, worked clearing acreage along the banks of the Licking River. As the men worked clearing trees and brush, they could never have imagined what the future would hold for the land on which they stood. James Taylor Jr. went on to be an important figure in getting the city of Newport and Campbell County approved through charter. Standing on the banks of the Licking River, Taylor would look out proudly over the land that was being cleared. His first views of the area held hope for a bright future. As time would tell, the fight to maintain that hopeful feeling would be challenged at every turn.

The use of slaves was a normal and accepted occurrence in that time. The rewards that Taylor gained from the work of the slaves were immense. It would prove to be the first example of the battle between good and evil on these hallowed grounds.

WRETCHED SOUNDS OF DISEMBODIED SOULS

After the settling of Newport, the population boomed, and soon even the outskirts of town were being developed. New residents began settling an area on the banks of the Licking River. As the area grew, Marcus Finch was tasked with plotting out the land. The area he plotted became known as "Finch's Subdivision." Eventually, the settlers in the new area called the place Finchtown. During the 1870s, a slaughterhouse was opened on the extreme southern edge of the property line that Bobby Mackey owns today. At the time, Finchtown was a small settlement complete with a hotel and two slaughterhouses. The small meatpacking business that sat on the property was called Winstel's Slaughterhouse.

For years, legend surrounding the club has been that the hole that remains in the basement is where the blood and refuse from the animals was funneled. This drainage ditch was connected directly to the underground runoff tunnels and would wash away the refuse into the Licking River. After much digging, however, I was surprised to find information that said otherwise. There was, in fact, a slaughterhouse on the extreme southern edge of the

An early map of Finchtown showing the slaughterhouse and distillery. *Courtesy Campbell County Historical Society.*

property. The small home that was used for slaughter was nothing near the scale of a commercial slaughterhouse. It was rather a local butcher who would offer slaughter service to local residents of Finchtown. The area of land where the house sat is several hundred feet south of the club today. As history tells us, the hole that remains in the basement of Bobby Mackey's today was used for an entirely different purpose, as we will soon explore.

During the years after the Civil War, the area along the banks of the Licking River was used to perpetrate revolting crimes. Southern whites were resolute in ending the voting rights of blacks. Furthermore, they were unhappy with the civil rights shown toward blacks following the completion of the war and the signing of the Emancipation Proclamation. Newport was home to many "hanging trees," where angry mobs would act out their lynchings. The area where these macabre trees sat includes the site where Bobby Mackey's sits today. According to a *Kentucky Post* article, the strip of land from Monmouth Street to the Licking River and then south was the site of so many hangings that it became known as "Gallows Gap."

As early as 1865, people reported encountering ghostly apparitions when passing through this region. The extreme southwest corner of the Newport city boundary, in the exact area of Bobby Mackey's Music World, was home to at least twenty hangings. The article makes a point of saying that only one hanging was done legally. This was also the area of the first public gallows in Newport, near the banks of the river.

People would report strange occurrences in this area, and some would wait until a train passed through to venture into this area, so as to not hear the wretched sounds of disembodied souls. Nearly 150 years later, the reports of ghosts in this area still persist.

Rockets in the Night Sky

As Finchtown continued to thrive, so too did its expansion. In 1876, work was completed on a sprawling set of distillery buildings owned by George W. Robson. The warehouse sat across Licking Pike, but the production buildings themselves lined the banks of the Licking River. As part of its production of whiskey, the distillery received permission to dig three tunnels below the train tracks that led out to the Licking River.

The tunnels were meant to serve two purposes. They would drain away rainwater that could possibly wash out the train tracks. Secondly, and more importantly, the tunnels were dug in order to pump water from the Licking River up into the buildings for use during the distilling process. The tunnel opening that remains in the basement of Bobby Mackey's today was one of three used to pump water into the distillery. Contrary to popular belief, it was not used by the slaughterhouse to wash away blood from the killing floor, but rather to aid in the production of whiskey. A little known fact is that all three tunnels still exist in the basement of the property.

The massive distillery produced large amounts of whiskey, with the warehouse readily holding twenty-eight thousand barrels. The business was known as Geo. W. Robson, Jr. & Co., later as Licking Bourbon Distilling Co. and finally as Old 76 Distilling Co.

On September 4, 1888, the citizens of Finchtown experienced a rude awakening when an explosion rocked the small town. At around 10:00 p.m., George Ulrich was making his rounds as the night watchman. Just as he entered the condensing room on the third floor, he was blown back by the blast. The force of the explosion collapsed the south wall of the distillery onto the boiler shed. Ulrich suffered horrific burns on his face and neck but ultimately survived the incident. Luckily, no other injuries were reported.

The distillery continued on with a successful operation following the explosion. Things ran smoothly until fire struck again on January 24, 1907. At about 9:00 p.m., the night watchman Henry Hampton came across the fire, which quickly began to spread out of control. As the fire grew, the flames spread to William Mittemiller's saloon and Nestley's Drug Store, which were also located on the grounds owned by Bobby Mackey today. Both the saloon and the drugstore were total losses.

To add insult to injury, the saloon and drugstore were looted before the fire overtook them. Residents scrambled to help carry furniture and valuables out of the buildings but kept walking and stole the items. The fire burned fiercely, gaining momentum toward the area where the barrels of whiskey were stored. The storage area was at maximum capacity. As the flames engulfed the storage area, the barrels of whiskey exploded like rockets in the night sky.

The only death that occurred was that of Louis Buerger, a Newport teenager who was known to have heart problems. When the fire broke out, he began running from his home at Tenth and Columbia in Newport out to the scene of the fire. During his run, Buerger fell to the ground, dead from an apparent heart attack.

The Old 76 Distilling Co. was eventually lost to Prohibition in 1919. The buildings, complete with all the distilling equipment, were sold off, and the massive structure was torn down.

Given the history of the site being home to saloons, nightclubs and illegal liquor during Prohibition, it seems fitting that the area was first home to a distillery.

CHAPTER 2

SCANDAL

Though the story of Pearl Bryan's murder is still sensational today, its link to the site of Bobby Mackey's Music World has come into question. According to popular legend surrounding the club, Scott Jackson and Alonzo Walling were involved in occult activity at the site of the old tunnel from the distillery. Some have theorized that the two were giving blood sacrifices to Satan there on the site. The fact remains that there is not a shred of evidence to support these claims. The distillery was in business during the time period in question, which squashes the theory of Pearl Bryan's head possibly being thrown into the abandoned hole in the ground.

Over the years, however, the infamous murder of Pearl Bryan has continually crept into the legend surrounding the haunting of Bobby Mackey's. There is absolutely no evidence connecting the site to the Pearl Bryan murder. We will, however, briefly cover the topic in order to give you the full scope of the legend surrounding the club.

At around 11:00 p.m. on the evening of January 31, 1896, Fort Thomas resident Josephine O'Brien heard the screams of a woman coming from the direction where a body would be found the following morning.

At 8:00 a.m. on the following morning of February 1, 1896, twelve-year-old John Hewling was cutting across the property of John Locke, a farmer in Fort Thomas, Kentucky. While passing near a ravine, the young boy made a horrifying discovery. Lying in a pool of blood was the lifeless, headless body of a woman. Too startled to investigate further, Hewling immediately ran to the farm and summoned the help of Mike Noonan, a workman on the ranch.

Noonan went to view the body himself and returned with the news to the farm owner John Locke. When the body was found, it was not damp. It had rained in the area the night prior until about 9:00 p.m. The body being found dry corroborated Mrs. O'Brien's story of hearing screams around 11:00 p.m.

After notifying Commander Colonel Cochran at Fort Thomas, officials started showing up, including Sergeant Phillips of the Newport Police and Coroner Tingley. Photographs were taken of the body and surrounding crime scene. The woman's dress was thrown up over her shoulder, and her corset had been torn from her body. A clean and bloodless clump of vibrant red hair was found on the victim. Upon further examination of the body, the coroner noticed that the neck had several jagged cuts that changed direction. The head was severed below the fifth vertebra. According to a *Kentucky Post* article, "The lacerated neck shows that the torture was inflicted with a hack-knife or other instrument not sharp enough to overcome resistances readily." While processing the crime scene, the coroner made a gruesome discovery. Blood spurts were found as high as six feet up into the surrounding trees. Blood was found soaked three inches deep into the soil under the body. The coroner concluded that because of the large amount of blood at the scene, the girl was most certainly alive during the beheading.

After the body was removed, two police detectives, Crim and McDermott, were sent to process the crime scene. When the two arrived, they were shocked to find the area flooded with dozens of gawkers, souvenir hunters and soldiers from Fort Thomas. The crowd was taking everything with blood on it, including tree branches and dirt. For a time after the murder, farmer John Locke allowed gawkers to pay him to visit the area where the body was found. He also charged ten cents for citizens to view pictures he had taken of the crime scene. Interest in the murder reached such sensational levels that locals soon began speaking of Mr. Locke's growing frustration with curiosity seekers. In order to keep his crops from being trampled, he eventually began lying to visitors about where the crime scene was and sent them in a direction away from his crops.

During the investigation, Arthur Carter from Indiana arrived with three bloodhounds to aid in the search for clues. The dogs found so many scents from the trampled area that they sent twenty men to jail as suspects. One scent that the bloodhounds picked up on led to the Covington Reservoir nearby. The entire reservoir was drained at the cost of $2,000. Investigators found nothing.

The body was put in the care of Undertaker W.H. White in Newport. National newspapers touted it as "the crime of the century," but police had little to go on. Upon hearing the news, a large crowd began to gather outside the morgue in Newport. Anybody who claimed to have any knowledge of a missing woman was allowed to view the corpse. The body was dressed in a green checkered housedress "of the very cheapest material," a blue flannel underskirt, black stockings and cloth-topped shoes. Because of the cheap clothing, many believed the woman was a prostitute who was visiting the soldiers at Fort Thomas.

Emil Ester and William Hess positively identified the headless body as one Mrs. Markland. The two found Mrs. Hart of Cincinnati, the mother of the victim. The mother and father came to view the body. Upon viewing it, they both broke down in tears. The mother said that the shape of the legs and breasts were the same as her daughter's, who had been missing since New Year's Eve. Police quickly tracked down the lead only to find Mrs. Markland alive and working in Cincinnati. Several other people positively identified the woman. Each time the police investigated, they found the person alive and well.

Finally, the police looked to track down a positive identification by investigating the size-three shoes on the woman's feet. The bottoms of the shoes were imprinted with "Louis Hays, Greencastle, Ind. 22-11. 62,458." The sales record revealed a purchase by a Ms. Pearl Bryan of Greencastle, Indiana. Twenty-two-year-old Pearl told her family she would be traveling to Indianapolis and had not been heard from since January 28. Upon hearing the news of the murder in Greencastle, Pearl's brother Fred sent a telegram to Indianapolis to reach her. When a telegram came back that she was not there, the Bryan family panicked.

Investigators brought the woman's clothing to the Bryan family in Greencastle to view. Being a prominent and wealthy family, police were unsure that the cheap clothing belonged to Pearl Bryan. As quickly as police unveiled the garments, Pearl's mother began sobbing uncontrollably. The dress, she said, was fashioned for Pearl from a dress that had belonged to her dead sister. To fully identify the victim accurately, police told the Bryan family of the unusual webbing between the toes of the victim. After a long period of lamentation, the family confirmed it was indeed Pearl.

Police hastily went to work and uncovered several telegrams sent between Pearl's cousin William Wood and Scott Jackson. Pearl had fallen in love with the dental student from Cincinnati. A short time before the murder, Pearl confided in her cousin that she was pregnant. Wood immediately sent a telegram to Jackson with the news. According to Wood, Jackson was enraged when he found out. The two men kept communicating, and Jackson soon began sending Wood various recipes of concoctions to give Pearl to induce a miscarriage. It is unclear whether Pearl took these remedies willingly or was given them secretly.

When police arrested Jackson, he asked if they had arrested Walling yet. At the time, nobody had heard of Jackson's young roommate Alonzo Walling. Jackson then began blaming Walling for more and more details that emerged. According to records, police did in fact include the area of the old slaughterhouse and distillery in their search but found nothing.

On the witness stand, embalmer W.E. Abbott testified that he found a puncture wound on Pearl Bryan's body. He said it looked like a hypodermic needle puncture and

A portrait of Pearl Bryan. She was murdered less than two miles from where Bobby Mackey's stands. *Author's collection.*

was caused while she was still alive. The wound was found on her left side between the fifth and seventh ribs. Further, he stated that the way the puncture looked was consistent with an injection of ergoline, a chemical used for vasoconstriction, or the narrowing of blood vessels and arteries. This injection would be used to limit bleeding during medical procedures.

During the autopsy, the medical examiner also found cocaine in Bryan's stomach. He testified that the amount in the stomach was enough to render a person unconscious but that cocaine is soluble within the body and more may have been present through absorption into the body. Jackson had purchased the cocaine, which was readily available, at Koelble's drugstore on Fifth Street in Cincinnati. On the night of the murder, Bryan was seen with Jackson and Walling at Wallingford's saloon in downtown Cincinnati. Jackson ordered a whiskey for himself and a sarsaparilla for Pearl. It is believed that Jackson may have drugged Pearl's drink with the cocaine at this time.

During the autopsy, Pearl Bryan's fetus was removed from her body and preserved in alcohol. The fetus wound up at the A.F. Goetz Pharmacy at the corner of Fifth and York Streets in Newport. The fetus was eventually taken off display for fear of being stolen and was lost.

DRESSED IN A GLEAMING WHITE GOWN

Pearl Bryan's headless remains had been kept at Forest Hill Cemetery for nearly seven weeks while the family held out hopes that the head would be found. Family members begged and pleaded with Pearl's heartbroken father to allow her remains to be buried without the head. "It must be found," he would answer. Finally, after some convincing, he came around and made plans for her burial. On the afternoon of March 27, 1896, the sun was shining bright in Greencastle. The brown foliage of winter was now turning green, and fresh buds abounded. The sounds of singing birds rang out through Forest Hill Cemetery as mourners gathered. Pearl was finally prepared to be taken to her final resting place.

The gathering included family, close friends and the officiating pastor, Reverend Gobin. The hearse carriage held a beautiful pure white casket adorned with only a silver plate on top. The plate was engraved simply

Bobby Mackey's stands as a reminder of what time can leave behind. *Author's collection.*

"Pearl." Inside the closed casket was Pearl's body, dressed in a gleaming white gown that she had worn during her high school graduation. The carriage stopped, and all was silent, barring grief-stricken sobs. As the doors swung open, Pearl's casket was met by her schoolmates from the class of 1892. The old friends remembered happy days gone by as they carried Pearl to her final resting place. The casket procession was followed behind by family, intimate friends, village people and a crowd of curious onlookers in the back.

At the request of Pearl's parents, a grave was opened at the highest point of the cemetery, within view of the home where Pearl had been born and grown up. Someone in attendance noted that just before her remains were consigned to the grave, the sunlight hit the silver plate perfectly, looking like "the glisten of a star on a cloudless night." With a few prayers, the body of Kentucky's most notorious murder victim was laid beneath the ground, out of sight but not forgotten. Over the years, the notoriety of the case continued to bring the curious to Pearl's grave site. Two headstones had to be removed due to vandalism because people were chipping away pieces of them to keep as souvenirs. Today, the grave is unmarked and bears only the base for a headstone. Many visitors still pass by her grave, leaving pennies heads up in the hopes that she will find her head in the afterlife.

THE TWO BEGAN VIOLENTLY THRUSTING

As the trial of Jackson and Walling concluded, the two were found guilty and sentenced to hang for their crime. Jackson was a twenty-eight-year-old with a thick moustache, and Walling was a baby-faced twenty-one-year-old whose involvement in the murder came into question from the very beginning of the investigation. As dawn broke on March 20, 1897, two coffins sat in the jail yard awaiting the remains of Jackson and Walling. At 7:35 a.m., Reverend Lee prayed with the men, and they sang "God Be with You till We Meet Again." While eating breakfast, a message came into the jail for Alonzo Walling. It was from his girlfriend and read, "Die Game," meaning to die bravely. After breakfast, Jackson looked out on the mass of people gathered, grabbed a chair and sang hymns to the crowd out his window.

Three minutes before the men were to be taken to the gallows, Jackson told Sheriff Plummer that he wanted to clear Walling's name. Jackson sat down with hands trembling and wrote a telegram to the governor that read simply, "Walling is not guilty of this crime. I am." The mayor came in and asked Walling one last time where the head was. Walling replied, "Mayor Rhinock, before God, whom I shall soon meet, I do not know. I will not lie now." The mayor replied that he needed more details to postpone Walling's execution, but Jackson clammed up. Mayor Rhinock wanted Jackson to tell him why Walling was innocent. "I can't say that. That's a trap. I can't say that without admitting I was there," Jackson said. He then stopped talking. Through tears, Walling continued, "Jackson can save my life if he will, but he won't. I have tried in every way to get him to do it, but he will not. He ought to save me."

The two men were taken to the gallows constructed behind the Newport Courthouse. Tickets were sold to the event. The men were led to the top of the scaffold just before 11:30 a.m. and were asked if they had any last words. Jackson turned his eyes toward the sky and spoke, "I only have this to say, that I'm not guilty of the crime for which I am now compelled to pay the penalty of my life." Walling was noticeably trembling, with his eyes staring at the ground below. He was asked if he had any final words. "Nothing," he said, "Only that you are taking the life of an innocent man, and I will call upon God to witness the truth of what I say."

The executioner then placed hoods over the men's heads. The nooses were placed around their necks. During an execution, the knot of the rope is typically placed just under or just behind a person's ear. This is meant to break the neck and snap the spinal cord with the force of the falling body. In the case of Jackson and Walling, the rope was too short to cause this quick and painless death.

At 11:40 a.m., the two men fell from the gallows. Because of the shortened rope, by accident or with malicious purpose, the men's necks did not immediately break. The two began violently thrusting as they slowly choked to death. The violent tremors and shaking went on for what seemed like forever. Onlookers were horrified and had to look away. By 11:43, Jackson's fingers stopped twitching. At 11:44, Walling gave one last violent movement of his shoulders and then went limp. The crowd had just witnessed a repulsive sight. Officials had botched the hanging. This was the last public hanging in Newport.

Stories attached to the Pearl Bryan murder become more blurred when entangled with Bobby Mackey's haunted history. There are stories of Jackson and Walling threatening to "haunt" the area after their deaths. There are also stories that Pearl Bryan's head may have been thrown into the old hole in the basement floor. These stories have no historical backing and simply aren't true. Nothing in the Pearl Bryan investigation included the finding of anything significant from the site that is now Bobby Mackey's. In fact, there are old newspaper articles touting the discovery of Pearl Bryan's head. The *Kentucky New Era* printed the following on March 21, 1896:

> *The head of Pearl Bryan, the Greencastle Ind. woman, who is said to have been murdered by Jackson and Walling, and who's* [sic] *body was found near Fort Thomas, a mile or two from Newport, Ky., has been found after a search of seven or eight weeks. At least a head has been found by the officers and a number of people who were well acquainted with Miss Bryan have viewed it, and they are positive it is her head—and the authorities feel sure that the people are right and that the last link necessary to complete beyond a shadow of a doubt the identification of the body found is now in the hands of the law.*

During the time when the skull was found, forensic identification was not yet evolved into the exact science it is today. Other newspaper articles reported the discovery of severed heads around the area of Newport, including one that was buried and one that washed up on the bank of the Ohio River. There is no way to know the fate of these skulls and certainly no way to discover whether any of them belonged to Pearl Bryan.

This sensational murder has etched itself into the consciousness of the area. Many visitors and paranormal investigators who have visited Bobby Mackey's claim to have made contact with the ghosts of Pearl Bryan, Scott Jackson and Alonzo Walling. Since the crime holds no ties to the property, is it possible that these encounters point to something much more sinister going on at this most haunted of nightclubs? Later we will explore the very real possibility that particular ghosts who have been spotted may be the harbingers of something incredibly evil—and not human.

CHAPTER 3

DOWNFALL

The area of Finchtown and Newport was growing rapidly by the 1890s. As the population grew, crews began building the infrastructure, including a new bridge between Newport and Covington.

False!

Just before 11:00 a.m. on the morning of June 15, 1892, a group of men were working on the new Eleventh Street Bridge to span over the Licking River between Covington and Newport. Carpenter Murray Reardon was speaking with foreman Frank Mure about the stableness of the structure. Reardon warned that the bridge was in danger of collapse. Mure simply laughed at the carpenter. Reardon reiterated his fear, saying, "I tell you that false work won't stand the weight of those girders. It shakes every time the traveler runs out. You can't drive piles in that river that will be secure."

Reardon left the conversation agitated and walked toward the middle span of the bridge. It was a giant formation of timbers trussed together with iron rods. The span rose 126 feet above the river, where Reardon now stood. Realizing he needed bolts, he began walking back toward land and the blacksmith shop. One of the workers attempted to call Reardon back, saying he had all the bolts they needed. "Never mind," the carpenter shouted back. "I've come this far, I might as well get them now."

He had barely reached the east pier when he heard the sound of cracking timbers. As they began to give way, the wood moaned loudly like a banshee through the morning air. The giant structure suddenly began to sway, and quickly the mass of steel began to crumble with a deafening roar. Cables broke loose and went flying in all directions.

Reardon and the men who stood safe beyond the middle span now watched in horror. What they saw would stay with them forever. Like a house of cards, the massive structure came screeching down until the entire span between Newport and Covington smashed into the Licking River with unbelievable force. The workmen let loose horrible screams as they plummeted with the wood and iron.

In an instant, fifty-four men were hurled into the murky waters of the Licking River. Their bodies lay tangled and bloodied among the twisted steel, some hopelessly pinned to the bottom of the riverbed as they slowly drowned or were crushed. Word spread immediately, and several workers from the nearby Licking Rolling Mill sprang to action.

As bystanders watched in terror, the water could be seen being churned by the unfortunate men who were trying desperately to escape the wreck from beneath the water. Some were merely twelve inches beneath the river's

The scene following the bridge collapse that killed forty-one. *Courtesy of the Kenton County Public Library, Covington, Kentucky.*

surface. As time passed, the rigorous splashing of the water went away as more and more men slowly drowned. Workers from the Rolling Mill gathered up bodies from the murky waters. Most of those retrieved were dead or dying; however, a few escaped with minor injuries.

One of the millworkers who assisted in the rescue was a man named E.A. New. He heard a cry for help from the middle of the river and immediately swam out to help the man. The man was sitting on top of the wreckage and above the water. When asked why he didn't jump and swim to shore, he told New, "I can't. My leg is caught." New tried to pull the man to safety, but the man's right leg was caught between two pieces of iron. Blood could be seen running down the man's leg, and again, New tried desperately to pull the man free.

The man now became more panicked, "For God's sake, pull me out!" New tried yet again with no success. "I can't get you out, your leg is caught," exclaimed New. "Then by God, cut it off. Take your knife, and cut me out. Do something!" the poor man yelled. "I've got nothing to cut you with. Wait, I'll give you another pull," said New. Just as he reached for the man's hand again, the wreckage began to settle. New shot back in horror and watched as the iron beams shifted from the man's leg and caught him under the chin. New moved to safety and looked on as the iron beams held the man's head between them and slowly pulled him beneath the water. The man sank deeper and deeper with a terrible look of fear on his face as he struggled. New was horrified to see the man thrashing and causing bubbles to come to the surface. The man slowly disappeared below the murky water. A few moments later, the water was again still without any sign of life.

As the bodies were pulled from the wreckage, they were placed on wagons. Horses darted away from the scene at full speed in order to transport the severely injured and dying men to boardinghouses where they could be cared for.

The injuries of those who were pulled alive from the ruins were unimaginable. Twenty-year-old William Roby was removed from the scene, his body completely mangled from the timbers he fell on. His brother Jack's body was also brought to a boardinghouse on Thornton Street. Jack's dead body had been pulled from the water. His widow screamed loudly at the sight of her dead husband. The screams brought William Roby back into a conscious state. "Don't cry, Annie, it hurts my head so," he said to his brother's widow. "Jack's all right, I hope, and I'm not going to die." William lay on a bed with his stomach and intestines missing from his abdomen. They had been torn away from his body during the fall, and he was slowly dying as a pool of blood dripped to the floor. Annie didn't have the heart to tell William that his brother was dead and let the boy die without learning the news.

News of the tragedy continued to spread across the region in the hours following the collapse. A neighborhood in southeastern Covington was known as "No Man's Land." It was said to be home to a collection of misfits with criminal records, where many carried sawed-off muskets as canes. The most prominent resident in the neighborhood was Johanna McNamara, who was extremely well known in police circles because of countless arrests for drunkenness. Her nickname was "Old Sis." The residents of No Man's Land were poor and did not immediately receive the news because they did not have telephone or telegraph wires.

When word finally came to the area, Old Sis was overtaken by the news. She had three sons who worked on the bridge construction. They were Jack (twenty-four), Frank (twenty-one) and Dick (eighteen). When the bridge went down, so too did the three young men. Upon hearing the news, Old Sis immediately began running in the direction of the catastrophe. She nervously began wringing her hands as she ran, fully consumed by grief and weeping loudly. When she finally arrived at Twelfth Street, her eyes saw hundreds of people who had gathered to watch or were working on the recovery efforts. She worked her way through the crowd while her loud cries echoed across the riverbanks. When she made it to the river's edge, a man who knew her and her sons reached out an arm and stopped her. "You had better go back, Sis, you can do no good. Jack and Frank are killed, and Dick is missing," he told her. Old Sis screamed in horror, "Oh, God! My darling boys are all gone now!" She fell to her knees, her uncontrollable screaming bringing others around her to tears. She was removed to a shady area beneath a tree. Following the accident, her three sons were buried as Old Sis watched, totally inconsolable. She had endured the greatest loss related to the collapse.

During the recovery efforts in the hours after the collapse, a seven-year-old boy walked up to the crowd. He witnessed the horrible injuries and the dead and dying lying everywhere. He wasn't noticed until he started crying. A police officer consoled the young boy. In one hand was a bucket of coffee and in the other was a basket of food the boy had brought for his uncles. The boy dried his tears with the hand holding the bucket and spilled coffee on his clothes. He had come with the coffee and food for William and Jack Roby, who as previously mentioned, had both succumbed to their injuries. The shaken young boy was given the news that his uncles were both dead. He was turned away and started back toward home carrying the awful news.

In the end, forty-one people lost their lives. The day after the tragedy, the *Enquirer* ran the story with the headline "False!" Many took this to mean that the stories spreading across the region were not true, but it rather referred to the false work on the bridge that led to the collapse. The Licking River had just seen the largest loss of life in its history.

The site where the bridge collapse occurred is merely a quarter mile away from the land where Bobby Mackey's sits today. With the shocking regularity of paranormal occurrences at the site, many different spirits' voices have been recorded of both men and women. Ghosts have definitely been known to haunt areas, residences or business around the area where they died. For this reason, it is certainly possible that some of the ghosts who call Bobby Mackey's home may hail from this tragic engineering disaster.

MASSIVE INTERNAL BLEEDING

According to deed records, John and Julia Popp acquired the property in 1931. The two-story building served as their home, a saloon and a bowling alley known as the Bluegrass Inn. From all accounts, John Popp had regular run-ins with local police. He was arrested for theft and other petty crimes and was widely known as Finchtown's notorious bad boy. As early as 1893, Popp was indicted by a grand jury for illegal gaming and selling liquor on a Sunday.

In 1919, Prohibition hit America. The Volstead Act, as it was called, banned the manufacture, sale and distribution of intoxicating liquor. While Prohibition was in place, it served only to fuel contempt for the law. Organized crime aggregates made millions, and the use of alcohol became increasingly accepted in social circles. Many common citizens now also had a means to make extra income through illegal intoxicants, and John Popp was among them. In April 1920, federal Prohibition agents armed with search warrants from the U.S. District Court in Covington descended on the Bluegrass Inn. Upon entering the saloon, the Prohibition agents seized wine and whiskey and arrested John Popp for illegal trafficking of intoxicants. The agents walked away with five bottles of "rock and rye"; a number of bottles of sweet, colorless liquor known as kimmel; and Italian wine and bitters.

Federal raids became more frequent in the years following the enactment of the Volstead Act. The small settlement of Finchtown was especially notorious for the availability of illegal gaming and liquor. In 1922, illegal vices were so common that federal Prohibition agents made plans to occupy Newport for the entire summer that year. The agents were finally beginning to make progress in the surrounding area, which also included a successful raid of bootlegger George Remus's multimillion dollar operation in Cincinnati. Colonel H.H. Denhardt oversaw plans for the long-term stay of the federal agents. Work was started in March 1922 on barracks that would house the agents and included officers' quarters, meeting rooms, mess rooms and bunks.

John Popp was once again arrested in March 1922 and charged with violating the Volstead Act by possessing whiskey and wine. It seemed as if a standoff was beginning, and neither the federal agents nor those responsible for the illegal practices would back down. Popp took an almost daring stance against the federal agents, continuing to possess and secretly serve illegal intoxicants at the Bluegrass Inn. The place was generally known as a speakeasy establishment with hidden gaming such as slot machines and readily available liquor. Agents again paid Popp a surprise visit on a Tuesday afternoon in November 1922. He was cited yet again for a large quantity of moonshine found hidden inside his establishment and ordered to appear before Oscar H. Roetken, the U.S. commissioner in Covington, on the charge of violating the Volstead Act.

The National Prohibition Act did not require states to take any particular enforcement action until 1929. In those early years, many violators simply paid fines and walked away free. In the area of Finchtown, Newport, Covington and Cincinnati, violations were so rampant that federal courtrooms were unequipped to deal with the massive undertaking. Slow and expensive jury trials were repeated again and again. The problem became so bad that the courts began offering "bargain days" when defendants could plead guilty for a light fine. As years passed, the enforcement fell more and more on the shoulders of federal agents rather than states. By 1929, over 500,000 people had been arrested under the Volstead Act, and federal criminal cases had quadrupled since 1916. Nearly two-thirds of prosecutions involved violations of the Prohibition laws.

For John Popp, paying the fines for violations was a smart business decision. He could bring in much more income from the sale of illegal liquor than he would pay out in fines. By 1929, the federal laws surrounding Prohibition had changed. Congress had adopted the "Jones Five-and-Ten Law." The penalty for first-time violators was now five years in prison, a ten-thousand-dollar fine or both. Popp's choice was now an easier one. He would shy away from the illegal liquor but continue to focus on his illegal gaming offerings. Slot machines had been a popular choice for nearly forty years in the area and were openly available at numerous locations.

Popp increased his gaming offerings in the hopes of replacing lost income from illegal intoxicants. In June 1929, however, after years of successfully beating the system and making large profits, John Popp was named in a Campbell County Grand Jury indictment of houses and places where slot machines were operating. He faced a large fine along with many others. Around this time, the beginnings of organized crime were sprouting up around Finchtown and Newport. In order to be successful, it seemed, the townspeople now understood that they must work together in order to overcome federal intervention and continue their profitable ventures. It was during this time that Popp employed a man known as Albert "Red" Masterson at the Bluegrass Inn. It was Masterson who ran most of the illegal operations taking place inside the Bluegrass Inn so as to keep the attention away from John Popp directly. As time would tell, Masterson would be connected to the building in the future in ways he could never imagine.

On Thanksgiving Day 1930, fire tore through the Bluegrass Inn. A $1,500 loss was caused to the restaurant and home. An overheated furnace was blamed for the blaze, which started in the first-floor hallway and quickly spread to the second floor. Popp had the building insured and quickly started restoring it.

After reopening, the site continued its profitable ways. Locals were well aware of the large profits the Bluegrass Inn took in. In the early morning hours of Friday, September 4, 1930, John Popp and his wife, Julia, were asleep on the second floor above the café room. At 3:30 a.m., they were awakened by the ringing of the burglar alarm. Popp and his wife ran downstairs to the café. In the confusion, Mrs. Popp grabbed a revolver from a dresser rather than the one under her husband's pillow. When entering the café, the two saw the burglar running toward the window, which he had broken to gain entrance. At close range, Mrs. Popp aimed at the intruder and pulled the trigger three times. The revolver failed to fire, and Mrs. Popp immediately discovered that she had picked up the gun with the broken trigger. The burglar exited the window and ran down Licking Pike toward Newport, leaving with nothing. Fate was on his side that night. Had Julia grabbed the proper revolver, he surely would have been shot.

In July 1933, two carpenters were working on Popp's building. The men were weatherproofing the outside of the building twenty feet above the ground when their scaffold suddenly collapsed. The men were thrown to the ground, where one man walked away with only a sprained ankle. Sixty-year-old John Beiting was not as lucky. He suffered massive internal bleeding from the fall and was transported to St. Elizabeth Hospital. He died a short time later from his injuries.

On the morning of March 1, 1937, alarms rang out at two Newport firehouses. Firefighters were called to a two-story building on Licking Pike. When they arrived, five buildings, including the Bluegrass Inn, were threatened by a growing fire. The blaze originated in an upstairs room that Popp had rented out to a boarder. In fact, Popp had several boarders living on the second floor above the café who were away at work that morning.

As firefighters fought the blaze, it gained considerable momentum on the second floor. Soon the roof collapsed, and Popp watched in horror as his business and home were slowly engulfed by flames. Crews were able to bring the fire to a standstill, but not before the Bluegrass Inn was deemed a total loss. Fire Chief Edward Miles estimated the damage at $4,000. In the end, only the brick walls of the building stood. The entire second floor was a loss, as was the café and bar on the first floor. For the second time in seven years, the Bluegrass Inn had suffered damage from a fire. The latter, however, was the final nail in the coffin for the Popps. They reopened the café once again but were no longer profitable. In November 1941, the café was broken into. The thief gained access through a window in the basement, where 375 packs of cigarettes and other articles were stolen. Shortly after, John Popp died, and his wife, Julia, sold the property.

After the successful but tragic years of the Bluegrass Inn, the site would see a revitalization and expansion courtesy of its new owner.

CHAPTER 4
FAMILY

The site was entering a new phase in which loyalties would be tested and the important players would be forced to rely on family to get by, whether it was family by blood or family by oath.

YOUR HONOR, WE HAVE REACHED A VERDICT

During the time when the Bluegrass Inn was turning a profit from the sale of illegal alcohol, many others were also profiting from the same practice. Two men who would later take control of the club were raking in enormous amounts of cash through the sale of illegal liquor on the black market. In Cincinnati, George Remus had set up the largest bootlegging operation in America. He was a force to be reckoned with. After moving from Chicago, Remus organized a sophisticated operation that involved him legally purchasing whiskey for himself for "medicinal purposes" and then hiring men to hijack his own shipments. The whiskey was then sold on the black market for up to $100 per barrel. Remus amassed a fortune, raking in an estimated $3 million in just two years (over $36 million in today's equivalent).

One man who worked for Remus was Earnest "Buck" Brady. Long before taking the reigns of the Latin Quarter, Brady laid deep criminal roots throughout the area and cut out his reputation as a man of success and stubborn control. George Remus would send shipments of whiskey out on the street, only to be hijacked over and over by one man. The man was so good at hijacking the whiskey that Remus decided to employ him. The ambitious man was hired by Remus to transport his liquor. That man was Earnest Brady. Better known as "Buck" among his friends, Brady quickly became a lieutenant for Remus. He was now in charge of a group of street soldiers responsible for transporting the whiskey safely for distribution.

At the same time, Brady was running the Stonewall House on Dixie Highway in Northern Kentucky. Using his connections with Remus to obtain whiskey, he began serving it illegally at the Stonewall House. In July 1920, Brady faced a jury after several operatives from the W.H. Jackson Detective Agency in Cincinnati testified that they drank ninety-eight-proof whiskey at the Stonewall House where Brady was the proprietor. In the end, Brady was slapped with a $500 fine and court costs. This would prove to be the first of many court appearances for the ambitious businessman, who would build the reputation of a successful nightclub manager, no matter what the cost.

After a raid at his Death Valley Farm in Cincinnati, the bootlegging empire of George Remus came crumbling to the ground. Buck Brady was among the men charged with conspiracy to violate the Prohibition law. He was captured in October 1922 when Prohibition agents attempted to pull over a caravan, including a truck and a car with Brady inside. A pistol fight ensued, with both sides sending bullets flying in all directions. None of those involved was injured, and the event ended in the arrest of several men. This clash would come to be known as the "Battle at Perryville." In April 1923, Brady's trial began. It was one of the quickest trials ever heard in the local court. During his initial arrest in 1922, Brady and colleague Lawrence Howard were driving behind a truck that was found to have two hundred gallons of whiskey inside. No intoxicants were found in the vehicle driven by Brady and Howard; however, the two were still arrested. The only fact brought into question during the trial was if Prohibition agents had the right to stop the vehicle Brady was traveling in during his arrest. After being found to be within the scope of the law, the defense had nothing. The prosecution rested its case, and it was announced that there would be no defense. According to an article in the *Kentucky Post*, "The case was then submitted to the jurors without argument." Brady was quickly found guilty, and bond was set at $15,000. In order to secure release on bond, Brady transferred the deed of the property where he lived on Seventeenth and Holman Streets in Covington.

In being found guilty, Brady was also hit with a $10,000 fine and sentenced to two years in the Atlanta Penitentiary. Brady was to report on February 2, 1925, to begin his two-year sentence in Atlanta. He didn't show. Instead,

Buck Brady, who was successful in every venture from bootlegging to nightclub management. *Author's collection.*

he took a twenty-six-day vacation with friends. He didn't surrender in Covington until March 1.

Word traveled quickly throughout Covington and Newport that Brady had returned and surrendered. A crowd of Brady's friends began gathering at the Covington jail. In fact, so many people showed up at the jail that Brady was permitted to have a "reception" in the Covington police courtroom. In an article in the *Kentucky Post*, Brady seemed coolheaded and calm. "I haven't anything to say," said Brady. "I just surrendered and am going to the 'can' to do a stretch of 19 months and 8 days." Having been sentenced to two years, Brady fully expected to be released early on good behavior.

Doing time with Brady was Lawrence Howard, a man with whom he formerly ran an automotive garage in Covington. He was also sent to Atlanta after being arrested with Brady and found guilty of conspiracy to violate Prohibition laws. Howard blamed Brady for his arrest and let those feelings of contempt wash over him during his time in prison. On the inside, Howard and Brady fought over who they thought should have taken the fall in the liquor arrest. During their time in prison, the two became enemies. Brady was released from Atlanta after serving fifteen months, and Howard soon followed him back into free society.

In October 1926, after being released from prison, Brady entered a police station at 7:30 a.m. saying, "I just shot 'Big' Howard, and I want to give myself up." Brady told police he was crossing the Fourth Street Bridge between Covington and Newport in his automobile when he saw Lawrence Howard on the Newport side of the bridge. "Howard shouted to me to stop my auto, saying, 'Come over here; I want to see you,'" Brady told detectives. He continued, "I stopped the auto. He started towards me. When he approached me he reached into his coat as though he was going to draw a gun. I drew my revolver and fired in order to protect my life." Later, Brady would say that he left his car and walked with Howard to the intersection of Fourth and Brighton, where Howard then reached inside his coat, and Brady fired on him.

Howard was shot three times in the abdomen, right leg and back. When investigators went to Howard's bedside in the hospital, he refused to give his name, address, any details of the shooting or name the person who shot him. Howard simply said, "Don't bother me, I'm in pain. Call a priest." When Howard was removed from the scene, he did not have any weapons on him. The only witness was a former Newport policeman. He testified that he found a loaded revolver near Howard immediately following the shooting.

Brady told police that Howard had made many threats toward him. He said that while they were both serving their term in Atlanta, Howard threatened that he would get him as soon as they got out of the penitentiary. He said that Howard had also threatened him over the phone on several occasions.

Lawrence Howard died several days after the shooting at St. Elizabeth Hospital. In December 1926, Brady went on trial for murder. At 9:30 a.m., the court came to session and took only thirty minutes to select a jury. Several witnesses testified that Howard had planned to kill Brady, one even recalling a scuffle inside the Atlanta Penitentiary in which Howard attempted to kill Brady with a butcher's knife. The state completed its case at 11:20 a.m., and the court adjourned for lunch. In a bizarre finish, both the state and the defense waived any final arguments, and the case was given to the jury by 4:10 p.m. They were given only two instructions about returning a death penalty verdict or returning a not-guilty verdict due to self-defense. Only ten minutes later, the jurors quietly ushered back into the courtroom. An anxious buzz overtook the courtroom as the jury spokesman said, "Your honor, we have reached a verdict." The verdict was handed to the judge and was read aloud. Brady was found not guilty by reason of self-defense. Forty-six-year-old Brady had once again survived a brush with catastrophe.

He Seemed to Have Exceptional Luck

Even through all the troubles, Brady continued to profit in the bootlegging business. In February 1930, Brady was arrested when trying to pass through to Canada from Detroit. A revolver, a sawed-off shotgun and ammunition were found in his vehicle. He openly admitted he was going to Canada to retrieve a shipment of whiskey and drive it back to Newport. He was slapped with a fine and continued his ventures.

Brady had many business ventures over the years, all with the purpose of making quick profits from illegal intoxicants and gambling. For a time, Brady ran a café at Sixth and Monmouth in Newport. After cutting ties with that operation, he ran a poolroom at 518 York Street. The establishment had three floors of dining and gambling, of which horse racing was a popular draw. Brady's place on York Street was so elaborate and so successful that other business owners in Newport became jealous of his success, and law enforcement attempted to shut down the operation.

Having built a reputation for being a killer, Brady continued to operate within the bootlegging circuit in and around Cincinnati. A feud among the area bootleggers was beginning to rise, due in part to territorial concerns. In July 1928, Brady was riding with his friend Joseph Johnson on their way to vacation in Detroit. The men noticed that they were being followed by a car with three men inside. As Johnson sped up, so too did the car following them. It soon became an all-out chase. Johnson and Brady sought refuge in the small town of Pisgah, Ohio. While being chased at high speeds, Johnson suddenly slammed his brakes, causing the pursuing vehicle to crash into his from behind. Stunned from the crash, Brady looked up to see the men outside the driver's window. One of the men pointed a gun at Johnson's head and fired, killing him. Brady scrambled to get away and ran into the Skinner Bros. General Store. As he entered the building, three shots were fired into the doorway. The shots missed Brady, and he found himself hiding inside the store until the shooters left the scene.

As police investigated the shooting, they were sure that the men were also planning to kill Brady in the exchange. With men trying to kill him, Brady agreed to help investigators in the search for the killers. He seemed to have exceptional luck, again escaping a life-and-death situation.

The year 1930 proved to be a trying one for Brady, who faced increasing pressure from Newport safety commissioner James Fuller. Brady's poolroom on York Street was raided, and twelve patrons were arrested. In court, he quickly posted a $250 bond and said he was "being picked on" by officials. Every other gambling resort in Newport was still open without the threat of being closed. A local newspaper reported Buck Brady's growing anger, saying, "Brady threatened to make matters disagreeable for other gamblers in the event he is not permitted to operate his establishment, declaring that if he cannot operate his place then no one else will run."

Brady was known as a smart businessman in many circles. In 1930, he was also overseeing operations of a club at 311 Licking Pike called the Green Lantern. Newport was heavily segregated, and the Green Lantern served as a gambling destination for black patrons. The games of chance and the money they brought in did not discriminate, and Brady saw to it that he received his share of the gambling profits brought in by area minorities.

STRICKEN WITH A MYSTERIOUS ILLNESS

In 1933, the nation was trying to shake the grip of the National Prohibition Act. After being found to be unconstitutional, the act was repealed. Things that were done behind closed doors for years were now once again legal. The many entertainment establishments around Newport that had worked so hard to hide their acts now openly offered liquor service. The rampant availability of illegal gaming continued just as before, and now patrons could legally become intoxicated without fear of retribution from local authorities.

Brady entered into a partnership with Mel Fernberg, who would later go on to operate other successful nightclubs in the greater Cincinnati area. The arrangement was short lived, and in September 1940, Fernberg filed a petition to the Campbell County Court asking for dissolution of the partnership between himself and Brady.

In the suit, Fernberg asked that someone be appointed to take charge of the property and its business administration until it was disposed of by the court. In addition, Fernberg asked for a restraining order against Brady and an injunction restraining him from withdrawing funds that were on deposit at the Newport National Bank. Finally, Fernberg asked for $25,000 in personal damages for the loss of future earnings and profits. In the suit, Earnest A. Brady, George S. Gebhart and Newport National Bank were named as defendants.

Mel Fernberg affirmed that on January 15, 1940, he became the owner and operator of the Primrose Country Club, which sat on the property that Brady owned. Fernberg said he operated the club until July 1, when he and Brady entered into an "oral contract and agreement." In this agreement, the two were to be partners in the operation of the nightclub in that Brady was to lease the real estate to the partnership for fifty dollars per week. Further, Brady was to have no part in the operation or conducting of business. Fernberg also said he was to receive exclusive use of the name "Primrose Country Club." For the leasing of the real estate, Brady and Fernberg would equally share all profits of the business.

Fernberg said that he had bought $1,400 worth of furniture and fixtures for the club on his own credit. After the purchase, Brady refused to pay any portion of the cost. By July, Brady told Fernberg he refused to lease the nightclub to him. Brady had cleverly allowed Fernberg to purchase all of the fixtures and furniture for the club and now wanted the business for himself. Fernberg alleged that Brady violated the terms of their verbal partnership agreement. He also alleged that Brady had continuously harassed him about the management of the club and interfered with regular business.

An advertisement for the Primrose Country Club. Pictured is Earnest Brady Jr. *Author's collection.*

Fernberg was being forced out, and he knew it. In the suit, he told of Brady's attempting to take over the business through threatening, intimidating and using acts of violence against him. According to the suit, an altercation occurred on August 31, 1940. Brady threatened the life of Fernberg and pushed him out of his ownership role. After that day, Brady began operating the business and collecting all the profits. During this time, Brady refused to account for any profits to Fernberg. It was this hostile takeover that prompted Fernberg to file suit against Brady.

Brady soon installed his son, Earnest Brady Jr., as manager of the Primrose Country Club and financed a complete renovation of the property. The Primrose reopened to rave reviews and looked to leave behind its reputation of being a rough-and-tumble nightspot. Brady Jr. was the face of the new-and-improved establishment, but his management duties would be short-lived. Brady Jr. was called away to duty in the U.S. Navy during World War II, where he was stationed in Fort Pierce, Florida.

In 1943, the newly renovated Primrose Country Club now served a much different clientele. As business boomed through 1943, everything seemed to be working like clockwork. A shocking event would soon shake the club and the city of Newport. After an argument one evening, patron William Davidson brutally beat a man to death in the men's restroom of the club. The fatal fistfight killed twenty-one-year-old victim Paul Goodhew. In newspaper articles, Davidson was described as a "dancer and gambler" and was wanted by the FBI for numerous crimes.

In the fall of 1944, Brady Jr. was stricken with a mysterious illness. He began suffering small aches and pains, a low fever, reduced appetite, headaches and extreme lethargy. After receiving treatment, he was released and granted a leave by the navy. On December 1, he suffered a relapse at home. Brady Jr. was soon diagnosed with tubercular meningitis. Tuberculosis bacteria had invaded the fluid and membranes surrounding his brain and spinal cord. The disease progressed in the blink of an eye, and he soon suffered through bouts of confusion, vomiting and seizures. Two weeks later, Brady Jr. was dead.

CHAPTER 5

UNRESTRICTED

Buck Brady had endured the loss of his son and was feuding with rival club manager Albert Masterson. Since the death of his son, Brady had moved to Florida and left behind the nightlife of Newport. It is unclear exactly what caused the feud between Brady and Masterson. On August 5, 1946, Brady was back in Newport, where he waited outside the Merchant's Club on Monmouth Street. Brady watched as Albert "Red" Masterson left to enter his Cadillac. After pulling away, Brady's vehicle pulled alongside Masterson's at a red light with three men inside. Someone was heard to say, "Hi, Red!" As Masterson looked over, Brady opened fire with a shotgun. It was the proximity that was the undoing of the attack. The distance between Brady and his target only caused the buckshot to spray and mostly hit Masterson's doorframe.

Masterson escaped from his Cadillac as it rolled away and crashed into other vehicles. He then quickly took cover behind a car. While attempting to flee, Brady also ran his vehicle into several parked cars. Having wrecked his car, Brady was forced to flee the scene on foot. He was later arrested while hiding in an outhouse and charged with disturbing the peace. Brady simply told the police, "When I hear shooting, I run!"

In the aftermath, Masterson lay in a hospital, having survived the attack. He knew exactly who was responsible. He and Brady were acquaintances since the days when the two worked for bootlegger George Remus in Cincinnati. When police came to Masterson's bedside to question him, the henchman remained stoic and held firm that he had no idea who shot him.

Masterson was the strong arm for the Cleveland Four, and the organized crime operation was going to handle this incident internally. Over the years, the popular lore surrounding this event was that Brady was being forced out by the Cleveland Four. The truth, however, is that Brady owned some of the land where the Primrose operated and even had apparent ties of his own to the crime family. The exact cause behind the shooting remains a mystery today.

Buck Brady went to trial for the shooting, while Masterson stayed true to the oath of mafia entanglement and said he could not identify Brady as the shooter. There was even a hailing back to their bootlegging days. During the trial, George Remus testified as a character witness on Buck Brady's behalf. Police eventually dropped the charges against Brady.

Brady owned much of the property that the club sat on until selling it to the Licking Realty Company and moving to Florida. The realty company then leased the property to Thomas Callahan, who began operating the Latin Quarter.

As mentioned earlier, the legend surrounding the club says Buck Brady was intimidated and pushed out by the mafia following the Masterson shooting. There is no evidence of this being true. If anything, the shooting forced him to lie low in Florida for nearly two years following the shooting. Brady had sold off his interest in the property and business in 1944. In that year, the club was renovated and was known as the Latin Quarter. A nightclub in New York was running at the time, also called the Latin Quarter. It was opened in 1942 by Lou Walters, father of famous journalist Barbara Walters. The New York club and Walters filed suit against management of the Latin Quarter in Kentucky, attempting to stop them from using the name. The suit eventually disappeared from historical documents, which leads to the assumption that a deal was reached, since the Latin Quarter in Kentucky kept the name for many years.

After the Masterson shooting, Buck Brady disappeared from Newport altogether. He didn't appear back on the Newport scene until 1948. In July of that year, he gained full control of the club by purchasing the property, the business and all shares of the Licking Realty Company for $100,000. The acquisition included all of the shares owned by Thomas Callahan and all of his interest in the Latin Quarter. He named his old bootlegging boss George Remus as vice-president. George Gebhart, who had worked at the property for fifteen years, was named general manager.

Brady's reign over the Latin Quarter was short-lived. In March 1949, he sold the club to Sam Gutterman of Cincinnati. Whether Brady sold out under pressure from the mafia is unclear; however, it was now being run by the Cleveland Syndicate through several frontmen. Brady sold for a reported $100,000 only eight months after purchasing the club. It is quite possible that an aging Brady was forced out by the mob at this point. The sixty-seven-year-old former bootlegger sold the property for the same amount he had purchased it for and retired to Florida. With Brady permanently gone from the picture, the mafia-controlled club continued offering nightly entertainment and illegal gambling.

What Gambling?

In September 1951, the Kentucky State Police sent in fifty agents to raid the Latin Quarter. Patrons and employees were arrested on charges of illegal gambling. Slot machines were confiscated, along with other gaming equipment.

During the winter of 1951, the nation stopped in its tracks to follow the Kefauver Hearings. Estes Kefauver chaired the Senate Committee to Investigate Crime and Interstate Commerce. The Tennessee senator set up a nationwide tour where subpoenas were handed down from New Orleans to Detroit to Los Angeles.

The focus of the hearings was to look into the inside workings of organized crime across America. Citizens were completely immersed in the hearings that were being broadcast into their living rooms. Bars began to fill with men who were there to watch the proceedings on their lunch breaks.

Powerful leaders in the world of organized crime, such as Frank Costello, were called to testify. One after another, criminals were called to the stand, where they were seen in homes all across America sweating and fidgeting nervously. Prior to the hearings, investigators for Kefauver's committee visited several nightclubs in Newport, including the Latin Quarter. The investigators witnessed nearly one hundred people gambling illegally, which included dice games and roulette wheels.

Lawmakers from Ohio and Kentucky were called and gave varying reasons for their lack of combativeness against gambling. Some said they simply didn't have the financial or manpower resources needed. Others claimed they were engrossed in other business, such as tax collection. One of those called in the hearings was Newport police chief George Gugel. When asked about what sort of gambling took place in Newport, Gugel answered

LATIN QUARTER BAR
BOLERO ROOM
FIESTA ROOM

Dinner, Supper Dancing and
Entertainment Nitely
Stars of Stage, Screen and Radio
3 Shows Nitely:
8:30 P.M., 12 P.M. and 3 A.M.

10 Minutes From Downtown Cincinnati

An advertisement for the Latin Quarter, boasting nightly entertainment. *Author's collection.*

The bar as it looked during the Latin Quarter days. *Courtesy of the Kenton County Public Library, Covington, Kentucky.*

simply, "What gambling?" Gugel played dumb and was just as ambiguous when answering questions as the others. Gugel, however, was doing more than just looking the other way. He attempted to prevent a raid while at Glenn Schmidt's Playtorium, where a press photographer pursued a photograph of him inside the club. Gugel took the camera, destroyed the film and had the photographer thrown in jail. He would later be indicted on corruption and conspiracy charges relating to the gambling taking place in Newport.

Elected officials not only knew about the gambling and prostitution going on in Newport, but many also received financial kickbacks for leaving the practices undisturbed. Nonetheless, despite the legal problems beginning to befall the area's clubs, they were still by all means thriving. And they certainly wouldn't go down without a fight.

Following the raid, increasing pressure was felt, and the club voluntarily closed the doors in January 1952. It soon reopened but then closed again in June. For five months the club sat empty, until November 1952 when it reopened. General manager George Gebhart booked a headline-grabbing set of entertainment that included Buddy Clayton, Helen Aimee, Franklin and Astrid, the Starlettes chorus line and Bob Snyder. The Latin Quarter was back, seemingly unscathed, and was bigger and badder than ever.

During the height of Newport's success, as many as 150 bars and gambling houses operated. This vast enterprise throughout the city was estimated to be bringing in nearly $25 million annually. Although there seemed to be enough money to go around, the competition was tough. To attract more customers and more of the money flowing into Newport, some businesses turned into full-fledged nightclubs, complete with dinner service and floor shows. The Latin Quarter was one that offered this unique and elegant mix of entertainment. The club boomed for years and became one of the most frequented in the area. Management of the club was known for sinking large amounts of cash into bringing quality music and vaudeville acts to entertain its patrons. Performers who graced the Latin Quarter stage included greats such as Nat King Cole and Ella Fitzgerald.

Today, remnants of those lost days are still apparent in several old cardboard signs from the Latin Quarter scattered around the club. Some signs boast nightly floor shows at 8:00 p.m., 12:00 a.m. and 3:00 a.m. Others tout $100 jackpots (nearly $1,000 in today's money) and the necessity of reservations. The club was firing on all cylinders and raked in huge profits. Some of those running the club, however, saw still more potential income from less-legal streams.

During its height, the Latin Quarter also offered gambling in the form of slot machines and other games of chance. The room where the mechanical bull sits today served as a casino for years. Old light switches still show specific labeling from those days calling the area the "casino room." Sitting quietly in a corner is a blatant reminder of these times. A small window opening still remains from the casino, a cashier's room where players would cash out their chips. Sitting behind the window is a small room that served as a cash cage, where stories have been told of men guarding the exchange of money with shotguns in hand.

Speaking on conditions of anonymity, a man who we will refer to as "Ed" spoke about the time he spent at the Latin Quarter during the days when the casino room operated. "The casino room was lined with all sorts of slot machines on the walls," he remembered. "And the cheapest you could get into one for was a nickel. Others took quarters, half dollars and a few even took silver dollars." When I asked about other games, he replied, "Why, there were different card games set up at a few tables in the middle of the room."

The casino room brought in as much money as all other parts of the club, if not more. Ed witnessed the way gambling would leave some patrons

A sign from the Latin Quarter showcasing cash prizes. *Author's collection.*

completely broke. "A lot of people went out of that place with no money left at all. They would go into the parking lot looking for a ride home or would hitchhike," he recalled with a smile. "And some guys," he continued, with a more serious look on his face, "would lose so much they would go after the dealer for a fight."

A view into the cashier's room, where gamblers would cash in their chips. *Author's collection.*

Legend surrounding the club says that the basement was used for interrogations and torture of those who were caught cheating the casino. I asked Ed if these stories had any merit. He quickly answered, "Oh, sure. Cheaters would take away the profits from the business, you see?" Slowly explaining with hand gestures, Ed continued, "Cheaters were dealt with quickly. Nobody wanted to see their money being taken away by some slick trickster. There was definitely violence involved, but the Latin Quarter wasn't the only place where this happened." When I pushed him further, asking if he knew of any murders that took place there, he gave a funny look and simply replied, "No." It seemed that even those willing to talk still have boundaries and are loyal to the famous vow of silence that lies at the core of organized crime.

When Brady ran the operation, he hailed back to his bootlegging days and ensured the club was stocked with plenty of liquor. For men looking to get drunk fast, Brady even offered moonshine in the back rooms of the nightclub. Having remembered the danger in transporting liquor from his days working for George Remus, Brady used the old tunnel from the distillery to transport the illegal intoxicants safely from a barge on the Licking River to the inside of the club.

After Brady sold his interest in the business, the establishment was mafia controlled. During the Kefauver hearings in 1951, the senator called organized crime families "syndicates." The moniker stuck. The Cleveland Syndicate was composed of former bootleggers Moe Dalitz, Sam Tucker, Morris Kleinman and Louis Rothkopf. They secretly continued operating illegal gambling ventures throughout Newport and Wilder.

Management of the club altered the staircase leading to the basement in order to make an escape in the event of a raid. The floor was patched over and a trapdoor installed. If a raid happened, the men could escape through the trapdoor, down to the basement and out of the club.

In 1955, Campbell County Police used sledgehammers to break into the club and confiscate an assortment of gambling equipment. Increasing outside pressure from opposing groups began to tighten the grip on the cash flow that the Latin Quarter enjoyed. In 1961, Newport's days of gambling glory came to an unceremonious end at the hands of the Committee of 500. The Latin Quarter was closed after the group successfully shut down the illegal gaming practices taking place inside the nightclub. The Committee of 500 was a group of business owners and residents who wished to stop illegal gaming in Campbell County.

The city of Newport now looked to take the community away from illegal vice and in the direction of legitimate business practices. Despite the blow, the Latin Quarter once again reopened for business. The landscape of gambling dens and prostitution disappeared altogether. The big players on Newport's gambling scene moved to Las Vegas, where they freely and legally pioneered the gambling Mecca known so well today. Back in northern Kentucky, some continued the practice of illegal gambling but did so in a much more inconspicuous way.

Buck Brady had retired to Florida, where his health grew increasingly grim. In 1965, the aging eighty-four-year-old walked down to the alley next to his apartment in Broward County. He then took his own life with a gunshot wound to the chest. The life of one of northern Kentucky's most revered characters was over.

The Latin Quarter began offering bingo inside the club. Management reputedly operated the bingo game for the benefit of a charity called the

Speers Society. A federal indictment came down on George Gebhart, the general manager of the Latin Quarter. The case went to trial, where FBI agents testified that the bingo game had been in continuous operation since 1964. The government claimed that accounting records compiled by the FBI from the Latin Quarter and the Speers Society showed a discrepancy in the net profit. They asserted that profits were being skimmed off the top for personal use.

The FBI testified that the Latin Quarter utilized several thousand bingo cards bearing the name "Bingo King Company, Englewood, Colorado." When the Bingo King Company was called to testify, it said that company records showed that orders were placed by George Gebhart. Because Gebhart placed orders outside the state of Kentucky, the indictment included charges of illegal interstate commerce on top of operating a game of chance. Gebhart lost an appeal in 1971 and faced an enormous fine and jail time.

With Gebhart out of the picture for a time, the mob knew exactly who they wanted to run the nightclub. David Whitfield was serving prison time when the Cleveland Syndicate took over operations. Whitfield was considered a suspect in the first Beverly Hills Club fire of 1936, which killed the niece of the caretaker. In order to secure early parole for Whitfield, the Cleveland Four gave a state authority $7,000 in cash as a consideration to make haste with parole for Whitfield. He was granted parole and immediately placed in the role of general manager at the club. The Latin Quarter was far beyond its days of glory. In the mid-1970s, the establishment halted operations for good.

The Bloody Bucket

Several years ago, I had the opportunity of meeting a gentleman who used to captain a barge that ran up and down the Ohio and Licking Rivers near the nightclub. We started talking about the history of the site, and he began warming up to me. "You're never going to believe this," he said to me, while looking around for eavesdroppers.

Speaking on conditions of anonymity, he went on to tell me of the days when he would bring liquor shipments to the banks of the Licking River at the shore near the building. At that time, the building was operating as the Latin Quarter. The men, he told me, would take the illegal booze up through the drainage tunnels and smuggle it into the club by bringing it up through the same hole the distillery used to pump water from the Licking River.

His face then changed from a smiling reminiscence to that of someone who just received horrible news. Lowering his voice and bringing his head closer to me, he continued. In all the time that he delivered the illegal liquor to the club, he told me, there were two visits that stood out in his mind. On both of those occasions, the men waiting for the liquor shipment also had something to load onto the barge. His eyes widened as he told me of the men struggling to wheel out fifty-five-gallon drums filled with concrete. The first time, he told me, there were two. The second time, there was one.

Then he looked me straight in the eyes and told me that he felt there may have been bodies in those concrete-filled drums. He was given only two instructions: take the drums down one of the rivers far away from the club and dump them, and don't ask any questions. According to this aging man, the men at the Latin Quarter did not want to know where he took the drums. He stated that both times he dumped them in the area of Hebron, Kentucky, where the Anderson Ferry operates. Our conversation then ended abruptly with the cliché "you didn't hear it from me"–type of goodbye.

One thing that has remained true among the men and women who were involved in the organized crime racket is that they take the oath of silence very seriously. Even those in their eighties and nineties refuse to speak about

Bullet holes of unknown origin are shown in this basement door. *Author's collection.*

what happened, either because they still fear for their lives or because they wish to forget.

After the Latin Quarter shut down for the final time, the building became a bar called the Hard Rock Café (with no ties to the national chain of the same name). During the days of the Hard Rock Café, the bar again garnered the reputation of being rough and dangerous. Some locals referred to the place as the "bloody bucket." According to locals, the nickname came from the fact that a mop bucket could be seen filled with mopped-up blood on most nights.

She Must Be an Escaped Mental Patient

One evening, a young Carl Lawson was working on clean-up at the Hard Rock Café. Heavy rain pelted the building. While performing his duties, Lawson was startled by a woman standing in front of him. He was sure all of the doors were locked. The girl giggled and said she was waiting for Robert Randall to come back for her. Lawson immediately took the woman for a lunatic. She must be an escaped mental patient, he thought. Carl told her that the bar was closed, and she would have to leave. The woman looked him in the eyes, smiled and told him she wasn't leaving until Robert returned for her. Lawson was not in the mood for games. He marched straight to the nearest phone to call the police. As he picked up the phone and turned back toward the woman, she was gone. Lawson searched the entire building for the young woman but found nobody inside and all of the doors still locked. The rough bar now included sightings of ghosts as well.

The violence at the Hard Rock Café escalated in November 1977, when twenty-year-old Richard Tonnies was shot in front of the club. He died from his wounds in January 1978. Violence continued when twenty-three-year-old Dan Groh was also shot in the neck with a shotgun and killed in an altercation outside of the club in January 1978. Following the death of Groh, Police Chief Robert Schindler closed the club as a public nuisance.

The building now sat empty, waiting in the shadows to reveal its gruesome past to some new, unsuspecting proprietor.

PART II
DIABOLICAL

CHAPTER 6

ACQUISITION

A car radio belted out a country music song as the vehicle slowed to a crawl outside an old nightclub, leaving dust behind it as it exited the highway. Bobby Mackey was in the driver's seat and his pregnant wife, Janet, the passenger. Bobby had loved country music since he was a child and had been performing for years in clubs in the greater Cincinnati area. In Bobby's mind, the time had come to choose whether to move to Nashville to further pursue his career or open up his own club near home.

The couple drove around the old building. Bobby was quite aware of what this place used to be. "I would drive past that building when it was the Latin Quarter and see all the cars parked along the road. I can remember seeing in my mind what the inside would look like all lit up," he recalls.

Bobby had seen the place prior to bringing Janet and felt a strange connection to it. "I felt like something was drawing me in from the building," he explains. He had no idea what dark history the site held. The couple pulled up to the back of the building, and Bobby implored Janet to take a look with him. While exiting the car, Janet suddenly saw something move on the staircase outside and watched as the door opened by itself. She asked if Bobby had seen it, but he replied that he had not. She instantly got an uneasy feeling about the place and followed Bobby inside against her better judgment.

Bobby wore a wide smile and was excited to share his find with Janet. The two entered through the door as Bobby began calling out for anyone inside. There was no answer. The young man and his wife soon found themselves to be entirely alone in the club.

The luxurious Latin Quarter dining room. *Courtesy of the Kenton County Public Library, Covington, Kentucky.*

Bobby made his way to the stage. His voice then broke the silence as he called out to a woman nearby. He claimed he saw a woman in a white dress walking through the club but then quickly changed his mind, telling Janet it was only his mind playing tricks on him. Bobby brushed off the incident and began to envision the club full of people who would come to hear his music. He couldn't have understood that what he saw would be the first hint of what was to come and would lead to endless terrifying encounters reported by employees, patrons and those closest to him.

From the first time she stepped inside the building, Janet had an uneasy feeling about the place. She begged Bobby to look elsewhere in finding a spot for his new venture. In the end, Bobby decided to buy the club, despite the pleading from his wife.

Shortly after beginning work to open his new nightclub, Bobby Mackey received a visit from a young man who lived nearby and said his name was Carl. Having worked at the Hard Rock Café prior to Mackey purchasing the building, Lawson was familiar with the building. Bobby Mackey remembers his first meeting with Carl. "If you ever need any help, I know all about this place," Lawson told him. Mackey soon hired Lawson as a handyman to help prepare the club for its grand opening.

As Bobby and Janet continued working diligently to ready the club for opening, Carl Lawson spent long days helping the couple with handyman jobs around the property. Inside the club, the hard work began to show as the place took on a fresh and new feel.

The sound of a broom sweeping the floor broke the eerie silence within the walls of the club on a sunny afternoon. Janet finished sweeping the floor and then entered the old casino room looking for Carl. He was nowhere to be found. Sweat beaded on her brow when instantly she was hit with a passing chill that wrapped around her like the arms of a stranger. She quickly became engulfed in fear when she heard the sound of someone whispering. Before she could compose herself, a ladder in the room began shaking violently. Staring at the unbelievable sight, Janet found herself deep in the grip of fear. The feeling of dread overtook her so entirely that she was unable to make her lips call out for help.

All at once, the ladder began walking itself across the floor toward her. The safety of her unborn baby now filled Janet's mind. Frozen with panic, she again heard a whisper. This time, however, the voice was clear. "Get out!" the voice warned. Just then, Carl came into view of what was happening. He observed the ladder walking intently toward its helpless victim. He overcame the anxiety caused by what he was seeing and ran purposely toward Janet. She put her hands up in an attempt to absorb the blow from the ladder. In the instant before the ladder fell on her, Carl grabbed her by the shoulders and pulled her to safety. The two were stunned to watch the ladder fall and cause a monstrous roar as it slammed into the floor. A tragedy had been averted, but the pair now understood the extreme nature of the spirits walking unseen around them. Whether the stories were true or not, Bobby understood that the stories of ghostly encounters could doom the club from the start. He made up his mind that he wasn't going to give up on his dream that easily and continued working to suppress the stories from Janet and Carl.

Shortly after the incident, Janet begged Bobby to abandon plans to open the club. "I had every penny put into this place," recalls Bobby, "and I couldn't have somebody telling ghost stories that kept people away." Bobby explains, "Where I grew up, if someone heard about a haunted house, they made a point to stay away." Bobby fully believed that Carl was telling Janet stories and "getting into her head." As time passed, however, he would begin to see the full power that the stories—or the spirits themselves—held.

The south side of the building, where the wing of living quarters was destroyed by fire. *Author's collection.*

The intensity of the encounters was growing. Just before Mackey was scheduled to open the club, a mysterious fire struck the building. The entire L-shaped south wing was destroyed. It was composed of several levels of living quarters where maids and porters had once lived. It also held a private poker room. The origin of the fire was never found.

Renovations of the club continued as the date of opening grew closer. One day, Carl and Janet were working in the old kitchen. During one of my talks with Carl, he recalled hearing strange things in the kitchen. "We would hear weird noises through the vents coming from the basement," he remembered.

While in the kitchen working, Janet once again came in contact with the dark forces at the club. She claimed she was grabbed around the waist and stomach by something. As the grip tightened, she tried desperately to wiggle free from the grasp of the invisible specter. She began to scream out in despair, and Carl once again came to her aid. When he entered the kitchen, Janet was let free by the force. "We heard evil laughter from all around us," Carl once told me. As the diabolical laughter encompassed them from all sides, pots and pans ripped away from the wall where they hung and flew across the room like bullets. Both Carl and Janet escaped without injury but were stunned.

Plans pushed ahead, and the club opened in the fall of 1978. Once again the rooms were filled with sprightly music and entertained guests. The malevolent spirits inside the club seemed determined to make crystal clear the fact that the building belonged to them. Soon others would begin to experience extreme showdowns, and the spirits would do whatever it took to make these new visitors leave forever.

CHAPTER 7

JOHANA

To understand the legend surrounding the club completely, we must also cover the topic of Johana. During the course of his terrifying experiences, Carl Lawson claimed to have found a diary inside the hole in the basement. He once told me that the book was labeled simply "Johana Jewell." Presumably, this was the girl's stage name. The journal told of her being a dancer in the chorus line during the days of the Latin Quarter. According to Lawson, the following series of events led to the discovery of the journal.

I CAN HEAR RAINDROPS BEATING AGAINST THE ROOF

On one occasion, Carl was standing near the bar when he suddenly caught a glimpse of movement in his peripheral vision. He immediately went into a combative stance and was frozen with fear. The apparition of a young girl with short blond hair appeared before him. She wore a full-length gown that reached her ankles. "My name is Pearl. I need your help," the frightening specter said. Carl continued to feel frozen with fear and worked hard to move his quivering lips. He asked her what kind of help she needed. In his mind, he wondered if this was all a trick with a sinister motive. Before she answered back, Carl said he heard evil laughter all around him.

In an instant, he felt the crushing blow of an unseen fist against his jaw. The blow was so hard that it would rival that of a professional boxer. Carl

The bar as it looks today. The "LQ" still exists on the flooring from the Latin Quarter. *Author's collection.*

stumbled backward in complete shock. Then another immense blow hit him in the ribs. He crumpled to the floor in terrible pain. At that moment, he felt the sensation of an electric shock emanating through his body. (This will be an important fact to remember later.) The attack continued with impacts made to his face and body. Soon, Carl lost consciousness.

When he awoke on the floor, Carl slowly regained his balance and made his way to his feet. He claimed to have seen an apparition behind the bar and was brought back into full consciousness when a number of loud gunshots rang out from the casino room. In a daze, he went in search of the source of the sounds. He hoped in his mind that this wasn't another trick to lure him into harm's way.

As he entered the casino room, it was filled with eerie silence. He returned to the bar to retrieve holy water he had brought with him. Just as he reached for the holy water, another number of loud shots once again rang out, this time from an area near the long hallway leading to the front entrance.

He listened carefully to the continued popping sounds. They were coming from a cactus decoration near the bar. He knelt down to inspect the cactus more closely. It was then that the cactus inexplicably split apart, and thousands of baby spiders sprung out, covering Carl's body. He sprung to his feet, screaming with intense terror as he attempted to smack off the tiny arachnids.

Carl ran quickly across the room, over the floor in front of the stage, and busted out of the back door. He made it down the staircase and ran across the train tracks and through the brush down to the banks of the river. He dove straight into the murky waters of the Licking River, hoping that the water would wash away the spiders from his skin and clothing. When he came ashore, he tore away each piece of clothing, inspecting it closely for any sign of the spiders. He saw none of them on his clothes or in the water.

Catching his breath and regaining his composure, he put his drenched clothes back on and went back inside the bar. He was amazed to find the cactus completely intact and undisturbed. The stunned man was exhausted and wanted answers.

What happened next was the result of an encounter he had with the ghost of Johana. He claimed that it was her ghost who told him to dig in the basement and look for a tunnel. He obtained a pickaxe and went to work on the floor, gouging holes with each swing. He soon made an opening big enough to crawl into. Pushing his upper body into the opening, he used a small flashlight to peer into the darkness. He was floored to see a hole in the ground. Perhaps, he thought, this was the tunnel Johana was talking about. Seeing that the tunnel was filled in, he looked around and saw another

The former casino room houses a mechanical bull today. *Author's collection.*

curious thing there in the darkness. A few pieces of paper lay inside the hole. He pulled them out and looked closer. Written on the pages were only a few words: "My name is Johana and I beg you to help me. I'm a prisoner in Hell. Search the spotlight room."

Carl next went upstairs to an area behind the stage. He looked up at a ladder that led to an area above the stage. The small door on the ceiling was locked. When he climbed to the top of the steps, he broke open the padlock with a hammer and slowly opened the creaky door. He ventured up through the hole and crossed the old catwalk above the stage. Totally engulfed in darkness, Lawson used a small light to illuminate the narrow walkway. Soon, he found another door leading into the spotlight room. When he entered, he used the tiny light to look through old artifacts and more of Johana's journal. He eventually found a handwritten note scribbled on the wall. This, he thought, must be what Johana was referring to in her journal. What he found written on the wall still remains there today and reads as follows:

My love is deep as the sea that flows forever
You ask me when will it end, I tell you never
My love is as bright as the sun that shines forever
You ask me when will it end, I tell you never

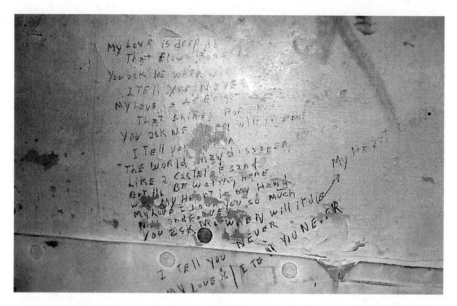

The poem on the wall of the spotlight room that is said to be Johana's suicide note. *Author's collection.*

The world may [disappear] *like a* [castle] *of sand*
But I'll be waiting here, with my heart in my hand
My love I love you so much, now and forever
You ask me when will it die, I tell you never
My heart cries out from hell
I will be waiting here
My love is / I tell you never

The journal that Lawson found inside the "well" in the basement and the other portion he found in the spotlight room contained stories of a girl named Johana, who planned to run off with her lover "Robbie." The man, Robert Randall, was said to have carried on a love affair with Johana that resulted in her becoming pregnant. According to Lawson, the journal of Johana held several passages referring to her relationship with Robert Randall. The following are excerpts from the journal:

Today is Tuesday. My father and I have had another argument. He told me to stay away from Robert. He said this would be his final warning. I don't know what I'm going to do. He said he would kill him. I would rather be dead than be without Robert.

It's after seven in the evening and I'm sick to my stomach. I've been vomiting every day for at least a week. I know what's wrong with me. I'm pregnant with Robert's child. If my father finds out, he'll kill me. Robert and I are going to sneak off together soon. We're going to Chicago where Robert has a friend who is a talent agent. He is going to get Robert a job singing in an all night Cabaret and help him pursue his singing career. We are going to get a small flat, and Robert is going to sing six nights a week. I don't want to keep dancing as a chorus girl. I need to find an easier job. Being pregnant, I won't take any chances.

We have to be careful not to let my father know where we're going. He would hunt us down and kill both of us. He's insane. My father would do anything to keep me from Robert. He said that Robert Randall was a no count bum. He always calls him by his full name. I call him by the pet name I gave him, Robbie. He laughs at me when I do this. We love each other so much.

Chorus line girls from the Latin Quarter. Johana is said to have been a dancer in the chorus line. *Courtesy of the Kenton County Public Library, Covington, Kentucky.*

It's Friday now. Robbie and I are going to sneak off after he sings his last song tonight. I have everything packed for our trip. I can't wait to get out of here. I want to get as far away from my father as possible. I can't believe the day has finally come for me to escape his cruelty.

Carl turned the page to continue reading. The handwriting that was so precise and neatly written on the previous pages had turned to an erratic collection of squiggles. The pages now had smear marks and appeared damaged by some sort of liquid. Johana, Carl thought, must have cried tears onto the page. The passages became more desperate. They are as follows:

I went to Robbie's dressing room and knocked over and over. No one answered, so I turned the doorknob and walked inside. He wasn't there. The blue shirt he had been wearing was on the floor, ripped all the way up the back. It was covered with blood. I know my father has killed Robbie. He'll rot in Hell for doing this. I don't know what to do. We were getting out of here. I'll never leave now. I'll kill my father and myself. I don't have a life without Robbie. This child inside me has no future without her daddy. I know it's a girl. I'm going to kill my father. He's a rotten, paid killer. He and Red have shot three or four men that I know of. They killed Tony in here two weeks ago over a lousy gambling debt.

When Lawson read the journal, he realized that he was getting a firsthand look into the prior days of mafia control over the site. Page by page, the diary told a story of love, betrayal and murder:

They took Tony's body down to the basement and carried him through the tunnel to the river. They don't think I know about the tunnel. They use it to bring illegal moonshine into this place. They think everyone is stupid. They get their bootleg whiskey sent here by boat up the Licking River. I can't believe they haven't been caught, all the times they have docked the boat and carried off stuff through the tunnel. Well, I'll see they get caught now. I'm going to write a letter to the government and tell them about the secret tunnel these fine upstanding men use at night. I'm going to tell them about the dead men they hauled to the middle of the Ohio River

The tunnel that was used by the distillery to pump water from the Licking River. Locals refer to it as "Hell's Gate." *Author's collection.*

and dumped overboard. I think they have buried some bodies in the basement. They filled in an old cistern with concrete instead of just covering it over.

I wish Buck was still here. He was a kind man. My father had Red run him off. They forced him to sell this place to their boss. They would have killed him if he had continued refusing their demands. If I knew where Buck was I would tell him everything I know about my father and his friends. I heard Buck tell my father he would return here someday and get revenge. Buck swore this place would never thrive as a gambling casino again. If there is justice, he'll return, and I sure hope he does. I'm going to take poison and leave this life after I poison my father. If there is life after death, I'll walk this place until my Robert returns for me.

This appeared to be the end of Johana's journal. The next pages were blank. Carl thumbed through the last pages and found one final entry. It is worth noting that this final entry is vastly more sensational and relies on the idea that someone dying of a fatal dose of poison would be in a state in which she could readily write out detailed facts while taking her last breaths. Since this journal ultimately burned in a fire inside the club, we are left only with the transcripts that Lawson kept of it. This final entry was indeed included in the transcriptions that Lawson provided of the journal.

There is a possibility that the entries are all entirely true. It is also possible that only some of them are true, while others have been embellished or remembered incorrectly. Lastly, it is possible that the entire journal was quoted incorrectly or entirely fictionalized. No matter the truth, or level thereof, it is important to include these journal entries to give you a complete understanding of the ghost stories and legend surrounding the club. Since many of the legends came from this final journal entry, I have chosen to include it here in its entirety. The final journal entry appeared as follows:

It's Sunday now. I don't have much time to write this down. I did it. I poisoned my father. I sat at the kitchen table and watched him pour three cups of coffee. He drank every drop. He always drinks four or five cups in the morning. I drank a cup with him. We are both doomed. The poison is working on me. I can barely see to write this down. My eyes are blurred. I waited until he fell to the floor. I told him I poisoned him and he was going to rot in Hell. He laughed and told me he had sold his soul to the Devil and he would be here forever. He said he would control me in death, as he has in life.

He told me the well was used as a gateway to and from Hell. I didn't understand what he was talking about. He said the well was a tunnel. He told me they found a sealed up well and climbed to the bottom of it. It was used to drain animal's blood into the river when the place was a slaughterhouse years ago. He and his friends dug from the bottom of the well toward the river, reopening the tunnel. He laughed at me and said he would return from Hell. He said he would keep Robert from me for all eternity. He said the Devil appeared to him in the well and he sold his soul for immortality. He will use the well to come back here.

He told me his friends would cover up our deaths just like they've done before. No one will ever know we existed. He told me the well and the Licking River [were] used for satanic ceremonies because it flows north just like the Nile River. That's not the worst of it! As

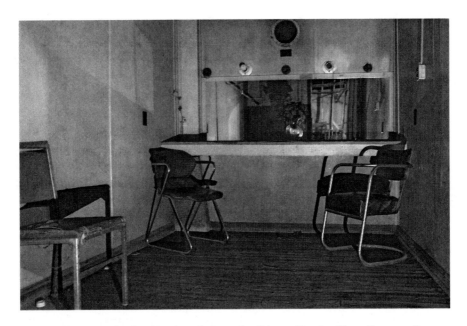

The dressing room that is said to have belonged to Johana. People still smell rose perfume here today. *Author's collection.*

my father lay on the floor dying, this spirit came out of him and identified himself as Alonzo Walling. He mocked me, saying it was he who entered my father's body and took control of him, making my father kill Robbie. The spirit laughed and told me he and his friend were hung for killing and beheading a girl named Pearl. The spirit of Alonzo said he would make all pregnant women who entered this place pay with their lives. He said it was his pal Scott who actually killed the girl, but he too was hung for the crime, and because of that, all pregnant women would suffer his wrath. He said Pearl's head was buried deep down in the well and that it was a blood sacrifice to Lucifer.

I'm going down to the basement and pray over the tunnel in hopes that I can block the evil from coming here again. To whoever finds this book, please find a way to seal the well and keep my father and his friends in Hell. You are my only hope. If my prayers don't work, I'll be his prisoner forever and many more people will suffer their evil wrath. I'll never be with Robert again if you ignore this. My father should be dead by now. My body is trembling from the poison. My mouth is so dry.

I don't have much time left. It's funny, I thought I felt my baby move.

It's raining outside. I can hear raindrops beating against the roof. I'm going to the basement and do what I can to stop my father and his evil. I'm taking the cover of this book and a few pages with me. If you have found this part of my diary, look in the basement for the other half. I'll try to write down what happens if I can. I'm looking at the words I just wrote on the wall. Please, Robert, come back for me. The words make me want to cry. I have to go now or I won't have the strength to walk to the basement. I can't wait any longer. Please help me. I need your help. My love is powerful. I'll find a way to come back and be with Robbie if you, whoever you are, will only help me. Please, I beg you to help me. If I fail, you must seal the well.

The legend of the old tunnel being "Hell's Gate" was born from the journal that Carl Lawson found. He would soon face the dark entities in a showdown that would test his faith and everything he thought to be true.

CHAPTER 8

DOMINION

J anet was diligently cleaning in the upstairs area that Bobby used for an office as the afternoon sun beat down on the building. Out of nowhere, she felt something grab her around the waist. "There was so much pressure and force, I could not get loose," she once recalled. She wiggled wildly, attempting to flee the grasp of the unseen force. She was picked up by the powerful spirit and brought back down to the ground. As quickly as it started, the grip around her waist disappeared. She ran for the doorway to sprint down the staircase.

Just as she reached the staircase and started down the stairs, something picked her up and she fell back up the staircase. Contrary to the popular version of this story, Janet was pushed *up* the stairs, not down. She gathered

The staircase leading to the upstairs apartment where Janet Mackey was pushed by an unseen force. *Author's collection.*

herself and moved to her knees. The invisible specter screamed at her, "Get out!" As a result of the incident, Janet went into premature labor and had her baby the following morning at 8:30 a.m.

HIS DEMEANOR CHANGED

After becoming overwhelmed by the terror and mental anguish he was experiencing, one day Carl drove away from the club heading south on Licking Pike toward St. John's Church. He drew an empty soda bottle from under his seat and took it inside the church with him. He crossed himself as he entered the church and went straight to the stand holding holy water. Carl filled the soda bottle, said a prayer and left the solemn calmness of the church and returned to his car.

He took the holy water to the club and sprinkled it over the old underground tunnel in the hopes of stopping the insane encounters. For a time, everything seemed quiet for a change. After the club opened, Lawson moved into the building as caretaker and turned the upstairs office into an apartment.

After several months, the quiet nature of the building was suddenly broken. While in the basement, Lawson came face to face with a horrid creature. Paralyzed with fear, the caretaker watched as the evil entity pointed a finger at him and screamed, "Get out now!" The hideous thing grabbed him by the throat and flung him into the air. Lawson struggled to get away, kicking wildly as he struggled to breathe. The creature slammed his body to the ground with enormous force. He struggled to catch his breath as the evil thing disappeared.

Lawson went again to the church to retrieve holy water. He went straight back to the club again with a soda bottle full of it. The toll of Lawson's experience showed in the form of exhaustion on his face. Inside the club, he encountered the despicable creature near the stage. This time he was entranced, staring deeply into the empty red eyes of the beast. Surely this isn't real, he thought.

An extreme chill passed through Lawson's body, and he became aware that he was floating a full five or six feet above the floor. When he came back to reality once again, he found himself firmly planted on the ground. Lawson ran out the back door and threw the holy water as far as he could. He was filled with a host of evil emotions. The demon was now in control of him, and his demeanor changed.

Carl Lawson, who fell under a demonic possession and required an exorcism. *Author's collection.*

Time went on, with Carl feeling like himself sometimes and not in control at others. The calm man was beginning to become aggressive and nasty at times. Carl began telling people he didn't feel right. He said he felt like something was inside of him and reported crawling feelings on and under his skin.

The stories continued from Carl and Janet. Finally, Bobby called in a minister in order to appease those who were frightened. Although Bobby did not believe their stories, he wished to put an end to their fears and show them there was nothing to be afraid of. The minister involved Reverend Glenn Cole, who counseled Carl about his experiences. The reverend became convinced that Carl had fallen under a demonic possession. The decision was made that the best way to help Carl would be to perform an exorcism on him. The battle for Carl's life was about to begin.

THIS BODY IS MINE!

On a warm August evening in 1991, Reverend Cole visited Carl at the nightclub with the intention of performing an exorcism. Carl was overcome by nervousness. It took considerable coaxing on the part of the reverend to convince Carl to go through with the ritual. The rite began, and Carl seemed at ease. Soon his personality changed, and he began speaking as other entities. Carl spoke loudly, referring to himself in the third person. He lashed out at the reverend, saying, "Ever since Carl was a kid, all he wanted to do was go to church and pray. But I got him riding around here on his bicycle. Carl's so stupid he didn't even know what happened to him!"

Carl Lawson adorned the door of his apartment with the words "Go Away" in order to keep spirits out. *Author's collection.*

Reverend Cole grabbed his Bible and showed it to Carl. "Stick that stupid book up your ass!" he exclaimed. The back-and-forth banter continued as Carl became more agitated. Reverend Cole was done trying to reason with the entity possessing Carl's soul. "By the authority of God's word," he asserted, "I command you to leave!" The reverend gripped Carl's hands tightly as he thrashed about and attempted to break free from the grip.

The rite continued on, and Carl fell back from his chair to the ground. Reverend Cole continued to command the spirit to leave Carl. Sitting on the ground, Carl slapped his chest as he repeated, "I don't have to go nowhere! This body is mine! This body is mine!" He got on all fours and hissed and growled at the reverend. From his throat came the sound of a thousand voices.

Reverend Cole once again grabbed Carl with a tight grip. He continued praying over the possessed man. Carl shook and thrashed violently, trying to escape the grip of God's warrior. The reverend prayed continually for what seemed like an eternity. Carl spewed out terrible shrieks and groans that came from deep in his abdomen. All at once, the thrashing and groaning ceased. The reverend continued to shout out prayers and commanded the spirits to leave Carl. After more than six grueling hours, there was an eerie sense of calmness that was overtaking the possessed man. All of the tense muscles in Carl's body went limp, and he jumped into the arms of the reverend. He cried loudly as he became aware of what was happening. "It's over," the reverend told Carl. "They're gone."

Carl gathered his wits and stood up and hugged the reverend, thanking him with sincerity on his face. He felt totally drained from the event. He went upstairs to his apartment to get the rest he so rightfully earned.

CHAPTER 9

IMITATION

Knowing full well the power they hold, the spirits that reside inside the nightclub can be aggressive and nasty. Some even seek to manipulate or trick investigators during their stays. One night while putting on an investigation event in the basement, something happened that changed the way I viewed the paranormal world forever.

During a session in the well room, just outside of the old jail cell the mob used, something amazing happened. It was amazing—and terrifying. While using a modified frequency-sweeping device, we began hearing strange voices through the speakers. Then the speakers went completely silent. After a few moments, a voice came through clearly without any distortion or other background noise. Everyone in the room heard this device say "Connie." Standing in amazement, nobody even got out a single word before another word came from the silence: "Cancer." At this point, everyone began feeling a little unsettled. I spoke for the group and asked out loud what this meant. The device went silent again. This time, however, we were all inundated with something none of us would ever have expected. Standing there, in the middle of the musty basement, we all suddenly smelled fresh-baked gingerbread cookies. Even by my standards, smelling a fresh batch of ghostly cookies sounds outlandish. But it happened, and we were all stunned and confused.

Suddenly a young woman began sobbing and was visibly upset. When I inquired what was wrong, she said to me that she had an Aunt Connie, who died of breast cancer and was known for making gingerbread cookies. She told me how she was simply amazed that her aunt was there with her. I

This small room was used to detain people during the time of the Latin Quarter. Demonic spirits have manifested in this area. *Author's collection.*

was forced to take swift action and remove the young lady from the investigation and take her outside. While outside I told her that her aunt Connie was not hanging out in a dusty old basement of a haunted nightclub and that she would certainly have picked another way to make contact if it had really been her. The woman looked confused. "That wasn't your Aunt Connie. I'm sorry," I told her.

These spirits, in their infinite and creepy wisdom, are known for mimicking or manipulating people. The negative ones, the evil ones, know things about you that nobody in the world could possibly know. And they will use that information to exploit you and break you down emotionally.

For this young woman, a startling encounter with a manipulative spirit could have spelled disaster. During my years of paranormal work and research, I've noticed a pattern with manipulative and negative spirits. The mimicking and manipulation is done for one reason: to open up an emotional connection to the person. And the people this happens to usually describe themselves as a self-admitted target. They are typically people who are not assertive or are credulous.

By opening up a person's emotions, the spirit has now made a connection, and it can lead to an attachment or worse. In general, but especially at Bobby Mackey's, I always give guidelines about what not to do. These are tactics you want to avoid so your chances of bringing home a spirit are diminished. Most people believe there is something inherently evil happening at the country nightclub. Many people are so overtaken with stories and claims that it's as if the place has taken on a life of its own. And that it has. The stories of terror and evil reach further than just to the geographic corners of the world. They have deep-reaching implications inside the human psyche.

HELP ME!

Although emotions can play a role in experiences, sometimes attacks occur for no apparent reason. In October 2011, I was preparing for a special event at the club. The event, called "Wake the Dead," would feature the One Man Electrical Band, better known as **OMEB**. A mix of dark music would be played to "wake the dead" and would be followed by an overnight paranormal investigation I would host after the club closed.

Mike Carr, the man known as **OMEB**, is a local celebrity on the music circuit. His classic hard-rock show is something to behold, as he performs spot-on renditions of rock songs complete with laser light show. One day, Carr was inside the club shooting a promo prior to the event. For a full thirty minutes while chatting with two others at the club, Carr says the audio recorded normally. The moment that Carr's friend Bob stepped on stage to begin the promo, however, the audio suddenly and inexplicably stopped recording.

The ghosts from Bobby Mackey's Music World are known for following people after they leave. *Author's collection.*

After finishing in the main bar, the men moved toward the basement to continue. Unaware of the extreme attacks that had been taking place down there in recent weeks, Carr and the others cracked open the door to reveal the dark and lonely basement. Work on the project continued in the substructure below the bar, and after completing his project, Carr remembered feeling a burning sensation on his neck and shoulders. "I thought I had pulled a muscle," he recalled.

He then returned to his studio to complete his work. When arriving, Bob asked Carr what was wrong with his neck. He had noticed something disturbing. On his neck, Carr had three distinct scratch marks, with one even appearing under his hairline. There had to be a rational explanation, he thought. Carr began intently reviewing the audio that was available and was shocked at what he heard. While listening to the recording a deep moaning voice was heard, sounding like someone who was in definite pain. A separate disembodied laugh also appeared on the playback. Carr found these voices to be disturbing, considering he is a practicing atheist. "I don't believe in an afterlife," he says. The most startling find for Carr was a loud, drawn-out whisper, begging simply, "Help me!" I have listened to these voices, and they certainly are not those of any living human.

Following his experience, Carr came face-to-face with the possibility that life after death was real. When asked about that possibility, he simply states, "I still don't believe in ghosts. But I believe there are other paranormal explanations." For some, firsthand experiences are the concrete proof needed to become a believer. For others, the reality of their experience brings about endless questions. For some, the experience lasts long after they depart the nightclub.

One such story took place in the 1980s when Steve Seiter was among first responders at an auto accident in front of the club. The doors of the club opened, and a woman with a full-length evening gown and light-colored hair came out with some red tablecloths to cover the bodies with. A man and a woman had died in the auto wreck. After an ambulance took away the victims, Seiter returned to the entrance of the building to thank the woman for her help. He found that the doors were locked, and nobody appeared to be inside. When he later told Bobby Mackey to thank the young woman, Bobby advised him that there was no way anybody came out of the club as nobody was there. He also told Seiter that he didn't have any employee even matching his description.

These strange experiences stick with those who have witnessed them long after the shock fades away. There are many hundreds of ghost stories originating from within the walls of the haunted club. For some, the aftermath of what they have witnessed is more haunting than the actual experience itself.

PART III
AFTERMATH

CHAPTER 10

PURSUED

Through the years since the club opened in 1978, one thing has remained the same. One constant has proven to bear fruit more than any other: people continue to have paranormal experiences. The way people perceive the club is also a constant. Patrons and outsiders alike view this sinister building as something time has forgotten, and sometimes they too wish they could forget their experiences.

What I experienced when I made my first trip to the infamous site was similar to what other people claim. I felt drawn to the place. It felt as if I had always belonged there. The sense of drawing I'm talking about is not a feeling of warmth and acceptance like at your grandmother's house. It's a forbidding feeling that, no matter how dark or extreme things get, you cannot pull yourself away. Bobby Mackey himself talked about this feeling during the days when he used to ride the train past the old Latin Quarter. Something about the building was drawing him in. "I would ride past the place at night and see all the cars parked alongside the road. It was all lit up, and I would imagine in my mind what it looked like inside," Bobby says. He felt a sort of belonging that many people report. "I never would have imagined that I would own the place one day," he continued.

Upon entering the building, it is easy to envision the way everything looked decades ago. Dinner tables would sit lavishly decorated with their chairs perfectly in place at the tables. The days of long ago almost beckon you to examine the ambience of those lost times. Today, the club still boasts many decorations from the days of the Latin Quarter. Simply look to either side of the stage where Bobby Mackey performs to see the original dancing ladies still hanging in the exact place they did decades ago. The floor near the bar is still adorned with a cursive style "LQ," a stark reminder not only of days past but also of those dark and black-hearted acts that were perpetrated during that time.

During the days of the mob stronghold over the Latin Quarter, Newport was a wide-open scene of gambling, booze, girls and gangsters. Mafia henchmen were known to use this area to hide out, leading to the nickname "Little Mexico." It was also during these days that the location where Bobby Mackey's club now sits saw its darkest hours. When the mob controlled the site, interrogations, torture and murder were commonplace in Newport. Much effort was put into covering up these acts, including bribing the local authorities to turn their heads the other way.

Today, the relics left behind provide a blunt reminder of just how different those times were. At its height, the Bluegrass Inn, Primrose Country Club and the Latin Quarter all offered illegal gambling on site. Evidence still exists today, including a window where players would cash in their chips. In this old cashier's room, it is said, men with shotguns would sit and watch over the exchange of money as it happened. Also in this room sits a grand-looking safe. It's straight from a Hollywood movie. Large and round, this massive

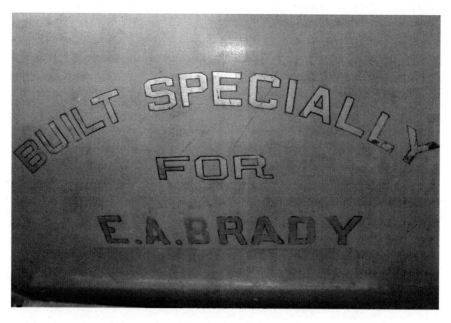

A large safe still remains from when Buck Brady ran the club. *Author's collection.*

safe bears the phrase, "Made specially for E.A. Brady." The man known as E.A. "Buck" Brady is the same man who oversaw the operation of the Latin Quarter for a time.

Through all of the claims of skeptics and cynics, one thing keeps popping up that they have no explanation for. It is EVP. With advances in technology, anybody with a simple recorder can simply push record and capture spirit voices. And people can do it with shocking regularity at Bobby Mackey's. Having been featured on countless television shows, the ghosts that haunt this nightclub are among the most famous in the world. And it is for this reason that the resident spirits seem to be among the most intelligent also.

Don't Trust the Light

During two episodes of Travel Channel's *Ghost Adventures*, the extremely dark side of the club was portrayed in shocking detail. Led by Zak Bagans, the *Ghost Adventures* crew also includes Nick Groff and Aaron Goodwin. Bobby Mackey's was chosen as the premiere episode for the series by the Travel Channel because of the trio's extreme findings.

After hearing stories of physical attacks, Bagans went straight to work on enticing the dark spirits. "Come and harm me!" Bagans exclaimed. While in the basement standing above the hole from the old distillery, Bagans continued, "If this is the portal to hell, why don't you come up out of the ground and come and get us?" Standing in the same room, Bagans began saying his back was burning. Upon inspection, three long and distinct claw marks were seen on his spine. It seemed that Bagans found the evidence he was looking for, but he never bargained for what happened following the investigation.

After their visit, Bagans, Groff and Goodwin all claimed to have experienced strange occurrences at their homes, such as faucets turning on, religious items being damaged and strange recurring dreams. Following their visit, Bagans went to seek counsel from Bishop James Long in Louisville. "You're playing with fire," he told Bagans. The *Ghost Adventures* crew visited the club twice more, including the filming of a second full episode for the Travel Channel. Each visit became more extreme than the last. Disturbing spirit voices were captured saying, "I'm gonna kill Zak," and "I'ma kill your wife." The men knew from their past experience that their exposure to these entities wouldn't end when they left. According to Bagans, he experienced a spirit attachment from Bobby Mackey's that took nearly a year to rid himself of.

James Long is the presiding archbishop of the United States Old Catholic Church. He was featured in both of the *Ghost Adventures* episodes filmed at Bobby Mackey's. Between the two episodes, the *Ghost Adventures* crew hosted a public investigation event in 2010 where fans of the show were invited to experience the haunting for themselves. During that visit, Bishop Long was in a room called "the room of faces" in the basement. The room has been adorned with this distinct name because legend says that a wall in the room has many faces that have appeared in it, possibly the victims of torture and murder from the days of mafia control. During the investigation of this room, Bishop Long encountered a force that certainly did not want him there. While standing in the room with his digital voice recorder, the bishop experienced a violent physical attack. "I felt a feeling like a very fast, strong flame on my hand," he explains. "It caused me horrible pain. The hair on my hand was actually burned, and you could smell it burning." The attack caused Long to drop his digital recorder on the ground, ruining it. Since the attack, he reports, hair has never grown back on the affected area.

For their second episode, the *Ghost Adventures* crew brought Long with them to participate in the investigation. He again experienced contact with

The room of faces got its name from the apparent faces that have appeared in markings on the wall. *Author's collection.*

extremely malevolent spirits. When they asked out loud if the spirits had evil intentions, they received a shocking response captured by their digital recorders. "That's because it's the Devil" was heard from some unseen entity.

The extreme level of interaction is certainly not a common experience for most paranormal investigators. Bishop Long is convinced that the property is home to demonic entities. When exploring the realm of inhuman spirits, common forms include animals, angels and what many religions call "demons." For some, the idea of inhuman ghosts might be a stretch. Simply put, however, it's no different than the diversity all around us. One must only look at the vast differences in race, religion and culture and understand that the same diversity exists in the spirit world. Long explains that demonic entities and demonic possession are not a new phenomenon. "They've always been there. The amount of people coming into contact with them has just increased due to the popularity of [paranormal investigations]."

While sitting in the dark in the room of faces, Bishop Long spoke out loud to any spirits present. "You have a clergy member alone, in the dark, so do something," Long said. At that time, a spirit voice was captured on audio responding, "Fuck you." Capturing these vulgar voices is a common occurrence at the club. Later while performing the Minor Rite of Exorcism, all of the men heard a disembodied growl. "It was a deep, drawn-out growl," Long recalls.

As the cleansing continued, another spirit voice was heard saying, "Don't trust the light." It was also during the cleansing that both Bagans and Goodwin became influenced by the dark energy present. At the request of the bishop, the men turned off the cameras and stopped filming. "Zak was in trouble," says Long, "and Aaron was really in trouble."

After his experience, Goodwin recounted his emotions from that night. In reference to the bishop, Goodwin admitted, "I wanted to kill him." The men were severely affected by the forces within the building, and their television show meant to entertain nearly became something out of their control.

It is understandably difficult for some people to believe extreme accounts like this. Without getting out there and experiencing these things for themselves, it can prove challenging to digest the claims of others. When asked about the extreme nature of his experience, Bishop Long made it clear that everything that aired from his visit was completely authentic. "I gain nothing from sensationalism," he claims. "I am not in business with Bobby Mackey or *Ghost Adventures*." He continued, "I can only tell you what we endured was 100 percent valid, and it was very, very intense." Dealing with paranormal matters is only one of the bishop's ministries. He isn't paid a penny for his work in the paranormal community. The calling has just become bigger than life, and he works diligently to educate people on paranormal matters and best practices.

Following the events that aired on *Ghost Adventures*, Long actually received complaints from paranormal investigators who were upset that they paid money to investigate the property but were thwarted by the recent exorcism and experienced nothing out of the ordinary. This shocking reaction goes to prove just how little some paranormal investigators understand about the real dangers they may encounter. Some paranormal enthusiasts contact the bishop to ask where to visit to seek out demonic activity. "I don't understand why people want to go to these places," he said. "They want the adrenaline rush, I guess." Long deliberately points out that it's not over after the adrenaline rush. "There's no question. It's just the beginning!" he exclaimed.

CHAPTER 11

CROOKED

There is no doubt that some of the otherworldly occurrences may be linked to the days of mafia entanglement with the club. It is certainly possible that the dark deeds of those days play a key role in what people are experiencing there today. The crooked dealings that have taken place at the site over the years might be the fuel behind some or all of the spirit encounters shared below.

THERE IS NO RATIONAL EXPLANATION

People travel from all corners of the United States to visit Bobby Mackey's, whether intentionally or when passing through the area. One paranormal investigator who is well traveled throughout the country is Tim Gavin from Alabama. He holds a passion for the paranormal world and openly admits his life is "strange." At two years old, he was clinically dead and suddenly came back to life. At five, he survived a horrific accident. Perhaps his close brushes with death have made him more in tune with those who have gone before him. "I grew up with spirits in my house," he says. Gavin has traveled the nation's countryside looking into mysterious occurrences in several states and is well versed in paranormal dealings. When visiting Bobby Mackey's, however, he noticed it had a different feel than the other haunted locations he had visited. "The energy inside that place is confusing," he says. Many visitors report a general feeling of uneasiness, a sense of dread or the feeling

Chairs sit in a circle inside the "Room of Faces." *Author's collection.*

that something just isn't right. According to Gavin, "It's draining, like being on a roller coaster six times in a row."

Having worked in law enforcement and narcotics investigations for twenty years, Gavin has definitely seen his share of criminal activity. But what happens when crimes of days gone by continue to haunt a location? More specifically, what happens when people who were players in an organized crime ring continue to call a place home even after they've died? "If a person was a gangster in life, that negative energy will still be there after they're gone," says Gavin. "There's a ton of negative energy in there. It feels like someone is on top of you the entire time."

During his visit, Gavin wandered into a dark corner of the basement, into a dressing room that is said to have belonged to Johana. While standing there in the darkness, he suddenly experienced the smell of rose perfume, which is a surprisingly regular occurrence. Just at that moment, he felt something brush his right elbow. Quickly turning around in the darkness, he illuminated the room with a flashlight but found that nobody was near him. Gavin had come in physical contact with some unseen force, as so many visitors report. Feeling physical interaction at this place is reported often by paranormal investigators and patrons. It's an unsettling feeling to know someone—or something—is around you that you cannot see.

I was with Gavin the night of his visit. We were packing up our gear in the middle of the basement when something startled us. With the lights on around us, a shadowy figure peeked around a beam very close to us. Before continuing, there is one thing you should understand if you've never seen something like this: *nothing* can prepare you for it. If you have never experienced seeing an actual "ghost," it's a difficult mix of emotions to describe. After the initial shock and adrenaline rush, your rational mind immediately tries to explain away what just happened. But when there is no rational explanation, the memory is logged in a sort of "I don't believe it!" limbo inside your brain. Many times on paranormal television shows you will see a person calmly telling the story of seeing a ghost, as if it's no big deal. People who have witnessed these things come across that way because although something amazing happened, it is sometimes too difficult to wrap our minds around. For this reason, these events are recalled quite matter-of-factly.

When asked about his approach to dealing with spirits, Gavin responded, "You must have respect. We do [investigations] for knowledge." Having a respectful demeanor is a necessary attribute for paranormal investigators who visit the club. Those who are disrespectful, as we've seen, usually regret their actions.

A Rush of Adrenaline

During an investigation of the nightclub while closed, Jeff Roemer experienced some strange occurrences. Being a retired law enforcement officer and veteran, he is not easily shaken. While inside the dressing room that is said to have belonged to Johana, all was quiet until his devices started to respond to a change in the environment. "They were going crazy," he says. He and the others in the room soon felt a presence, that innate feeling that someone else was there with them.

After a short time, the group left the dressing room. Roemer popped his head back into the room and took a photograph on his full-spectrum camera. When he saw what he had captured, a rush of adrenaline washed over him. There in the photograph was an apparition. It appeared to have shoulder-length hair, a protruding nose and even faint eyes and a mouth. Was this the ghost of Johana? Also in the photograph, a strange sort of curving anomaly is seen on the left side. It looks as if it is the "veil" opening up to expose this

Jeff Roemer captured this peculiar photo of what appears to be a face in Johana's dressing room. *Courtesy Jeff Roemer.*

figure. Nevertheless, the photo is strange. What would cause this figure to appear in the photo between Roemer and the dressing room wall?

On another occasion, Roemer remembers one girl getting the scare of her life. "We were sitting in the well room, and a camera flipped off a stool," he says. Startled by the camera falling forcefully from its perch, the girl shot up and ran for the door. The poltergeist phenomena continue to happen around the club today.

SOMETHING WASN'T QUITE RIGHT

Dale Hamblin is a former police officer and private investigator. On one occasion, he encountered the dark forces before even beginning his investigation. "We were still setting up equipment," he remembers. While standing outside the room that houses the old tunnel in the ground, he says he felt something strange. "My calf started burning," he says. When he lifted his pant leg, he saw two claw marks etched into his skin. "There wasn't anything around me that would have caused it," he states. "It's totally unexplainable. I've never experienced anything like that before." Without any provocation or irreverent attitude, Hamblin had been targeted and physically attacked.

His experience didn't end after his visit. After returning home, something wasn't quite right around the house. "My wife and I were sitting watching television, and I saw a picture frame on top of our entertainment center move by itself," he explains. Other strange occurrences befell him after his visit, such as a TV turning off and on by itself. What Dale experienced has become an all-too-familiar event for those who investigate the club.

What Did I Just See?

While conducting an investigation of the club on one particular night, I was accompanied by Becca Wilson. She works as a special education teacher by day and searches for signs of paranormal activity by night. While doing some EVP work in the room of faces, we began hearing what sounded like a man talking out in another part of the basement. Standing in the doorway leading to the main hall, I called out to whomever we heard. "We can hear you," I said. The talking abruptly stopped. We now heard only silence in the cavernous basement.

Becca slowly walked out of the doorway toward the area where the talking had been heard. She used a flashlight to look through the darkness. Suddenly a startled sound escaped her lips. While using the flashlight, Becca saw a man staring back at her, expressionless. She had illuminated his body from the chest up with the flashlight. Quickly she dropped the flashlight toward the ground and tried catching her breath as I asked her what was wrong. Thinking it was probably an uninvited human visitor, she again raised the flashlight toward the man. This time the man was nowhere to be seen.

Visibly upset and shaking, she worked hard to regain her composure. She remembers, "The man was very thin. He had short hair and very light-colored eyes, almost white." I had not seen this apparition, thankfully. What she had seen, however, was the clear form of a person. We searched the basement only to find nothing out of the ordinary. "He was about the same height as me and had big ears," she recalls.

As she relived the encounter with me, her eyes grew wide with the surprise she felt that night. "I was asking myself, 'What did I just see?' and 'Was that real?'" The ghostly man, she says, stood no more than six feet in front of her.

On another occasion, Becca says she experienced some very unpleasant touching by some unseen spirit. As she entered the room with the old tunnel from the distillery, she felt something pull her hair. Without acknowledging what just happened to her, she moved away from the area. She then felt a brush on her neck, which slowly moved down her chest. At that point, she felt a disturbing uneasy feeling. Becca had encountered ghosts before and used her strong resolve to once again brush off the unwanted interaction.

Moving into the room of faces, she soon felt a brush against her arm. "I thought it was a bug," she says. While standing in the room of faces, she felt yet another touch. This time she knew there was no possibility of it being a bug. "Something brushed my inner thigh," she explains. That night, the light touches continued on her arms and legs. "I felt like someone was trying to irritate me," she says. While driving away from the club that night, she felt something pull her hair in the car. "Something pulled my hair so hard, it came out of the pony tail," she remembers. Driving farther and farther away from the club, she felt ready to be done with the relentless touching.

For some reason, Becca is a regular target for physical interaction while at the club. During another investigation in the basement, myself and a small group of people watched in amazement as the necklace on her neck moved around by itself. Somebody or something was messing with it. She happened to be the only person that night who wore religious medallions, which hung on her necklace. This went on for several minutes as we all watched the clasp on the back of her neck move up and down, back and forth. It was as if someone was trying to unclasp it. Doing her best to maintain her composure, she stood still as we all watched in amazement and exclaimed things like "Oh my God!" After a few minutes, she had enough and left the basement. Upon leaving the damp substructure, the touching ceased.

Experiences like the ones mentioned above are only a few of the hundreds, if not thousands, of claims to spill from the club by paranormal investigators. Having gained worldwide notoriety, the spirits have become increasingly intelligent. And as we will soon see, they have learned to use this intelligence to let visitors know just how much they despise them.

CHAPTER 12

DECEPTION

With endless paranormal enthusiasts visiting the nightclub, the spirits have taken on personalities of their own. And they aren't personalities that want company. Spirit voices captured at this site go beyond the cliché "get out" responses heard at many haunted locations. They have been known to be nasty, and at times, they will outright lie to you.

SPIRIT STALKER

I did a walkthrough of the building in June 2009 for the Travel Channel's *Most Terrifying Places in America* and captured a shocking EVP that still stands as one of the best, clearest spirit voices I've ever taken away from the place. While standing near an old bathroom area next to Johana's dressing room in the basement, I captured the now-infamous "spirit stalker" EVP with my friend Chris Dedman. The chilling voice was used in the production of the Travel Channel's show, and our reactions to the voice were caught live as we heard it for the first time.

To me, this voice was very straight to the point: we were bothering him. I have been called a lot of things in my life, but being called a "spirit stalker" by an unseen spirit takes the cake. This voice haunted me for months after I first heard it. In the time following this capture, I also began collecting other frightening spirit voices of a similar nature. After a while I was completely

The area of the basement dressing rooms where the "spirit stalker" EVP was captured. Author's collection.

sure that the "spirit stalker" EVP was no fluke. Fellow investigators and I began capturing voices such as "Get them out of here" and "Die!" Still more were of extremely vulgar nature or even sexually explicit. These spirits didn't want company, and they most certainly were not playing around.

Chris Dedman has investigated the club on several other occasions, and it seems each time he visits, his experiences grow increasingly malevolent. He works as a paranormal investigator and lectures at conferences on the dangers involved with paranormal research.

On his first visit to the club, he worked with a thermal imaging camera, which measures temperature signatures in the environment and outputs them to a screen where possible anomalies can be viewed. He approached the "staircase to nowhere" and went left through the door at the base of the steps. Soon, he was totally embraced by darkness and watched intently as the thermal imaging camera gave him a view of what was happening.

What he saw next shocked him. "It was wild!" he said. There on the camera output screen was the shape of an apparition from the waist up. "It turned and looked at us," he said, "then went up the old stairs." The old stairs he speaks of still exist in the bowels of the basement from some previous incarnation of the building, most likely the distillery. Floored by what he saw, Dedman continued to explore the building searching for signs of otherworldly spirits.

In the room of faces, he explained how he encountered the spirit of an African American man. "At first, we could hear him humming a tune," he explained. "Then while using the ghost box, we heard the same voice answer us by saying, 'Yessah sir.'" Wanting to make sure that what he was hearing was real, he asked the spirit for an extremely obvious sign to prove that it was indeed him. Standing in the dark, Dedman and others waited anxiously for their sign. Suddenly out of the silence came the deafening rumble of a nearby air compressor. Upon closer inspection of the device, he was again bewildered at what he saw. "When we looked at the compressor, it was unplugged!" said Dedman. Perhaps he encountered the spirit of an unfortunate victim of the many lynchings that took place on the site.

During one visit, Dedman came in contact with the malevolent force that I have encountered several times. Across from the hole in the ground in the basement is a small room that was used as a holding cell during the days of mob rule. From within this room, Dedman said he heard a deplorable

The entrance of Bobby Mackey's is home to a sign that warns patrons of the building being haunted. *Author's collection.*

disembodied growl. Those who have experienced these vile growls will tell you how it made their skin crawl.

During another investigation, Dedman was on the main floor near the bar when he heard a loud noise from the men's restroom. "It sounded like someone was slammed against the wall or a heavy door slammed," he said. In the exact area of the men's restroom, the old "staircase to nowhere" used to open up near the old kitchen. During the days of the Latin Quarter, management covered the staircase with a trapdoor and would use it as a fast means of escape in the event of a raid on the club. Is it possible that what he heard was the old trapdoor being slammed closed? There's no telling, because today the staircase lies under the floor with no way to access it.

During his last visit to the property, Dedman reported the feeling of extreme illness while in the basement. Things had turned very dark in the days before his visit, with vicious attacks and malicious spirit voices being reported. The attack on Dedman, however, would not come in physical form but rather on a mental or spiritual level.

Taking a break from the building, he drove to a nearby gas station. "The farther I got away from the building, the better I felt," he said. When he returned, the feeling of overwhelming illness once again enveloped him. The dreadful feeling was so intense, he decided to call it an early night and go home. "By the time I got home, I was fine," he recalled.

I asked him if he believes that something inherently evil resides at Bobby Mackey's. His reply was instant: "Yes, I do believe that." He said he doesn't believe it is from any supposed satanic worship or the false connection with the Pearl Bryan murder. Instead, he believes that the evil within was either brought by someone to the place, or the generally negative past has caused energy such that may attract malevolent beings to the site.

I WASN'T ALONE

Over the years, I've met with a number of individuals who refuse to investigate the nightclub. Their explanations range from "I hear people bring ghosts home with them" to simply "It's evil." Even some of the most hardened paranormal investigators choose to stay away. In the same respect, sometimes skeptics visit the club and come away with things they just can't explain.

Rick Velasquez is a writer and documentary filmmaker. While filming a documentary about the club, he experienced several things that gave him an uneasy feeling around the property. Velasquez said his views on the paranormal aren't so cut and dry. When asked if he is a believer, he responded, "I think 'ghosts' are more of an energy left behind that resonates." He believes that ghosts can't necessarily communicate, but rather, he said, "I believe it's energy that plays on a loop."

While working on the documentary project, Velasquez and his fellow crew members walked through the basement. "I got a feeling that I wasn't alone," he admitted. In the room of faces, he said he encountered something he can't fully explain. "Everyone was walking out of the room, and I felt a hand touch me across the small of my back," he said. "I looked around right away, but nobody was near me." Unable to decipher what he experienced, he left the club with the feeling that some sort of energy was certainly there.

A portion of his filming included poking his head up into the catwalk area above the stage, which leads down to the old spotlight room where Johana's supposed suicide poem is written on the wall. The area made him more than a little uneasy, he said. "When I was pointing my camera down that catwalk in the darkness, I felt like something could pop out and scare me at any moment," he explained.

I asked him what would be causing the paranormal activity at the club. "I believe if there's any explanation for what's happening there, it [stems] from the mob days," he replied. He said that what he felt around the property was unmistakable. "I can't ignore what I've experienced," he said.

The many experiences that have been reported have continued even after several blessings and exorcisms performed on the site. In order to win the battle once and for all, the root cause must be found.

CHAPTER 13

MALIGNANT

Finding the root cause of the haunting at Bobby Mackey's has proved to be a difficult task for the clergy who have tried to cleanse the site of its unholy specters. As we will soon see, the rules in the battle between good and evil aren't always so clear.

BE CAREFUL WHAT YOU WISH FOR

Shortly after Bishop Long performed the exorcism shown on *Ghost Adventures*, paranormal claims once again began being reported regularly. "I could do a thousand exorcisms, and unless the root cause is found, it will continue," he explained. He points out that certain things contribute to perpetuating the level of paranormal activity, such as people who go in the building attempting to make contact, those who have spirit attachments themselves, people who openly invite spirits in or negative energy alone. Then the whole cycle starts again.

Don't believe in demons or that they can hurt you? "A demonic entity's presence or willingness to attack someone is not contingent upon someone's belief. Belief does not create them. Either they exist, or they don't. I know for a fact that they do," Long says.

Belief is a topic that also comes up when people engage in conversation about the possession Carl Lawson experienced. Since it is freely available on

A sign still remains from the Latin Quarter that advertises floor shows until 4:00 a.m. *Author's collection.*

YouTube, many have viewed the exorcism and questioned its validity. Bishop Long says that people certainly have the right to judge whether or not the exorcism looks "real." From his experience in having performed twenty-six exorcisms, however, Long says the classic Hollywood "look" isn't what a real exorcism is. "People expect to see a person flopping around like a fish out of water, but that's not an exorcism," he says.

During the taping of an episode of *The Geraldo Riviera Show* in 1992, the host spoke of the legend of satanic worship that may have occurred at the site. The fact remains that there isn't one shred of historical fact that links the site with satanic rituals. The tunnel that still exists in the basement was being used to pump water into the distillery for the purpose of producing whiskey. So if the claims of demonic worship are unsubstantiated, then why would these dark beings be present at this country music club? Bishop Long claims that negative residual energy alone can be enough to attract malevolent or demonic entities. "When you have that extreme negative residual, you have to be very careful with what might be present," he declares.

It seems that paranormal investigators receive regular interaction at this place, no matter who they are attempting to contact. "Demonic entities will certainly trick you into communicating with them," said Long. "Investigators always want to find out who it is. That's like going out in the ocean and looking for a great white shark. When you find it, and it becomes aware of you, you're a meal."

Long said one form of trickery contrived by demonic entities is to take on the image of an innocent being, such as appearing as an apparition of a child or using a child's voice.

While producing the second *Ghost Adventures* episode at Bobby Mackey's, some things were intentionally left out. "Some of the recordings were so sensitive, they didn't air them," the bishop said. "It was very emotional after that night, and it directly affected the lives of each of those guys." After the first visit, Aaron Goodwin admitted that whatever he brought home had been haunting him and was a major factor in ending his marriage. At times, the dangers last long after the investigation is over. And this is definitely one of those places.

Generally speaking, Bishop Long offers some advice to help paranormal investigators in their endeavors. "Don't provoke. Stop provoking," he begged. "It makes no sense to me. People are hoping to get evidence. They think when they get the evidence it's over. It's not." Long explained, "When you provoke, saying 'come hurt me,' or 'come scratch me,' the demonic entities are saying, 'Oh, I will...just on my time.'"

If you are looking to *not* experience an encounter with any demonic entity, Bishop Long offers some suggestions for your EVP work. "Ask preliminary questions, such as 'Do you believe in Jesus?', 'Do you live in the light?', 'Do you believe that Jesus is the son of God?', 'Do you confess that Yahweh is your god?' and so forth," he explained. A demonic entity will never confess these things, he said.

According to the bishop, one aspect people don't realize is when provoking demonic entities, they provoke back. "Be careful what you wish for," he said. "They work on their own time, not yours."

As a final reminder to those involved in paranormal investigations, the bishop beseeches everyone, "Stop picking up the Solemn Rite and performing an exorcism. This isn't my rule; this is the rule in the rite itself. The rubrics in the rite clearly state that only a validly ordained priest may perform this. Right before Jesus told his disciples to cast out demons, he breathed the 'holy spirit' upon them. That's called ordination. He ordained them first. Then he said go out and cast spirits."

According to the bishop, this has become a very bad problem. Laity are going around telling people they've been trained by clergy to perform exorcisms, which isn't true. "Some people are even claiming to perform exorcisms over the phone or on Skype," he asserted. From the things that I have witnessed, I will definitely leave the extremely dark and demonic side of the paranormal world to clergy.

Bishop Long holds a doctorate of ministry, a master's in education, a master's of science and management, a bachelor's in communication theory and an associate's of philosophy. "If I did not know for a fact that demonic entities existed," he said, "I would be doing something else with my time." The paranormal ministry has become an important one to the bishop, who claimed, "People need and definitely benefit from this help. I know what I have seen, and I can't ignore that."

Marked by Demonic Forces

One way demonic entities trick you into communicating is portraying themselves as innocent beings, as covered earlier. It was this tactic specifically that led to a long and destructive demonic attachment that I experienced in 2009. While regularly investigating the club, fellow researchers and I began capturing spirit voices eluding that they belong to a child who was murdered on the property. We even captured the name of "Timmy" while exploring communication.

This story is not one that I readily share with just anybody. I certainly don't like the idea of being viewed as a sensationalist looking for attention. Being a few years removed from these events, however, I now believe it's important to share my experiences in the hopes that it may save someone else from the same terror and feeling of helplessness.

I became infatuated with this child spirit and thought about it day and night. I would mull over in my head how sad it was for a young child to be forever trapped in a location. Over a period of a few months, these interactions continued. Each time we would offer the help of a priest, the communication would cease.

It was also during this time that I experienced one of my most extreme encounters at the club. While performing an investigation during hours in which the club was closed, I saw something that changed me and reaffirmed my belief about the spirit world. While standing near the bar in a small group of people, a woman with us said, "Do you see that?" and pointed toward the bull room. Sitting there in a chair was a man. His figure was illuminated only by the ambient light from the bar, since all the lights were off in the area he was sitting. Just as I looked to where she was pointing, the man moved slightly in his chair. All the hair on my body rose up with instant chill bumps.

His face had the most terrifying eyes that were glowing white. They moved with his body as he shifted in the chair. I could tell only that the man was wearing an orange shirt. I fumbled to gather paranormal detection equipment with the others who had just seen the man also. Fighting the urge to run out of the place, I steadily walked with the others toward the area where he was. After gathering the gear, however, he was nowhere to be found when I looked back.

As we entered the area where the man was, we saw nothing. A few of the devices we carried showed wild fluctuations for a few seconds and then went quiet. I breathed deeply, trying to recover from the scare that shot through my body.

A few weeks after the sighting, I met a person at the club who had old Polaroid photos from the days of the Latin Quarter. It must have been near the end of the Latin Quarter days because they were in color. In one of the photos, a singer and chorus line girls were pictured. The girls wore vibrant green dresses, and the man singing wore a bright orange shirt. I immediately thought back to the man I had seen. I will never know for sure, but perhaps it was the ghost of a singer from the club. Or perhaps it was something much darker.

Soon after I saw the ghostly man at the club, I began experiencing strange things at my home. Objects would dematerialize and disappear. I hung up my favorite shirt in the closet one night, planning to wear it the following morning. The next morning, however, the shirt was nowhere to be found. Only an empty hanger remained. I was perplexed. A few weeks later, the shirt reappeared in plain sight in the middle of a staircase in the house. This continued, with random items disappearing and reappearing in strange places. Then the events escalated.

After hosting an investigation event one night at the club, I woke in the morning and went to the computer to do my daily routine of returning e-mails. As I sat at a desk, the television ten feet away from me turned itself on. I had become used to the strange things happening, but this was extreme. I watched in disbelief as the channels changed and then stopped on an input that was only snow and static. I continued to watch as the volume numbers on the screen then turned all the way up to a deafening roar of static. I got up from my chair and quietly turned the television off without giving any response. I knew this wasn't some sort of prank, because I was alone in the home. As I went on with my business, it once again turned on. This time I flew up from my chair purposefully and went straight to the back of the television and unplugged it from the wall. That ended the strange events— for that day. The television never did that again.

As time went on, I began hearing the squeaking and cracking of the wood floors as someone walked around unseen. These sounds occurred when nobody else was in the house, or they were on another floor. While lying in bed one evening, I was in a relaxed state thinking about my plans for the following day. Out of the black stillness of the room, I heard something peculiar. It sounded like the door handle to my bedroom was being turned. The house had metal doorknobs that would squeak when they were turned. I looked down over my feet at the door, and the sound stopped. As my eyes adjusted to the darkness of the room, I focused in on the door and blew it off as nothing.

I laid my head back down and stared at the ceiling, again going through my activities for the next day. Then suddenly I heard the sound again, but louder than before. This time the doorknob actually turned, and the door popped open. I could see the ambient light pouring through the hallway window but saw nobody outside the door. Well, nobody I could see. I sat up from the bed and walked over to the door and looked out into the hallway. The house was again silent, and nobody was there. I tested the door to see if it could somehow pop open from a change in pressure or any other explainable circumstance. When the door was closed, however, there was no way to open it other than physically turning the doorknob.

Unexplainable things continued happening around me, and I did my best to ignore them. In the beginning, things happened at random times of the day and night. As things progressed, more and more occurrences happened in the middle of the night.

One night while sleeping, I awoke to the sound of footsteps and movement inside my bedroom. I was only half awake and not fully aware of what was happening. Something suddenly sat on the bed and caused the blanket and sheets to depress into the mattress. My girlfriend had experienced the sounds and the feeling of someone sitting on the bed as well. She yelled at me and told me to "get rid of it!" This one instantly gave me the creeps, and every hair on my body stood on end. I glanced at the clock. It was nearly three thirty in the morning. I stood up from the bed and shook my hand at the darkness, telling whoever or whatever was there that this was our house and they were not welcome. As a side note, demonic activity has been known to spike at 3:00 a.m. or come in threes such as scratches when a physical attack occurs. This is said to be a mocking of the holy trinity, in most religions known as "the Father, the Son and the Holy Spirit."

The encounters were happening more regularly, and I would soon find out that the reach of this demonic being went even further beyond my home. My entire life would soon be affected.

A laundry list of bizarre things starting happening around me. Car batteries would die when I was around, a water main burst at a place where I stayed overnight and a laptop computer and a desktop computer crashed and died, to name a few. During this time, my grandmother passed away, which left me vulnerable emotionally. It became abundantly clear that something was going on outside the realm of "normal." The things I was experiencing were unmistakable. There was no logical explanation for most all of it.

I felt that someone—or more appropriately, some *thing*—was spending a lot of time and energy to make sure I knew it was around. In the fall of that year, I was a vendor at a paranormal conference called Scarefest in Lexington, Kentucky. While at the conference, I sought out Bishop James Long for counsel. I briefly explained what had been happening. While standing there with the bishop and three of his priests, a wind blew past us inside the hall. Bishop Long looked to his fellow clergy and asked them, "Do you smell that?" They agreed, and Bishop Long told me it was a holy scent. A smile filled my face, and I asked if that was good news, that somebody is watching over me. "No, that's bad," said the bishop. "Tell me more about what you've been experiencing."

I gave more details, and the bishop told me quite frankly that I may be experiencing a demonic attachment. It was then, and only then, that I fully understood the scope of what had been happening. The bishop prayed over me, and I realized for the first time in two decades of paranormal research that I had gotten into something very bad.

Over time with prayer and protection techniques, I was able to rid myself of the sinister attachment. It took nearly a year. Some members of clergy claim that a person can be "marked," with a sort of spiritual bounty on his head, after experiencing a demonic attachment or possession. The reason given is that the demonic entities know you can defeat them and will continue to work to win the battle. I have been told that I am marked by demonic forces and have pretty much been begged to not return to Bobby Mackey's.

Bobby Mackey had no idea of the club's past when he purchased it in 1978. *Courtesy Bobby Mackey's Music World.*

The question I am asked most often after sharing this story is, "Why do you go back?" My answer is simple. At this point, the *only* reason I return to the place is to educate others on the real dangers of the paranormal world. Those who go there to enjoy music or a few adult beverages don't really have too much to worry about. The danger comes when paranormal investigators visit and make contact with the spirits there.

The second question people usually ask is how they can avoid taking home spirits or experiencing an attachment. In my eighteen years of seeking out knowledge on the paranormal, one thing sticks out as something that can lead to an attachment.

My advice is when you're hearing stories of tragedy or receiving spirit communication about something particularly emotional, do not share any of your own emotions. It sounds cold, but taking a sympathetic approach is much safer than an empathetic one. Sympathy is an understanding of how something feels. It's being able to relate with a person or situation without directly experiencing any of the associated emotions. Empathy is actually feeling the emotions that go along with an experience. From years of seeing patterns, it seems as though people who are empathetic and share those emotions open themselves up for a spirit attachment. With demonic entities, for example, they will use deeply personal information or portray themselves as a familiar family member who has died. In this way, they go straight for your spiritual throat with their tactics. Whatever your deepest emotional scar is, they will use that to attack you mentally or spiritually in order to open you up and make you vulnerable.

On several occasions while investigating the nightclub, I have captured an EVP about "Sir." The instances of capturing voices speaking of this "Sir" are always accompanied with the sickening smell of sulfur. This awful smell is commonly associated with the activity of inhuman spirits. During one investigation, a psychic was accompanying us. Without being given any information, she walked in and almost immediately mentioned the inhuman entity. She said that this would probably sound strange, but there was an entity there known as "Sir" whom the other spirits feared greatly. As she looked around, she rubbed her arms as if she was chilled by some unseen wind. "Sir is a demon," she told me.

I have met many people over the years who tell me they hope and wish that they could experience a physical attack or a spirit attachment. To them, I say, you're insane. Some people just don't understand the implications of going through something like that. For some, the experience lasts a lifetime. For all, life is never the same.

CHAPTER 14

POSSIBILITY

From voices to apparitions and noises to physical attacks, the site is home to some of the highest-level paranormal occurrences in the world. So why then does it happen here, on this site? Is it the vast number of atrocities that have occurred here? Is it that the spirits are somehow trapped here and are unable to cross over into the afterlife? Is the activity influenced by the large number of thrill seekers who come here from across the globe to catch a glimpse of something extraordinary? While we may never know the answer, there are specific properties the site holds that may point us in the right direction.

Bobby Mackey purchased the club in 1978 and ran it successfully for fifteen years. After this time, he purchased the Light Café next door and had it torn down. Mackey planned on building an entirely new club on the strip of land. Plans were drawn up, and he received zoning approval from the city of Wilder. To level the ground, Mackey brought in tons of dirt. The project saw construction delays due to spring rains and severe summer storms. In June 1993, a crack opened up in the earth. "All of the sudden, the earth just opened up," Mackey told reporters. The crack ran straight through the area where the new club was planned. The city recommended a geotechnical exploration of the site.

Some that know the history of the site today may say that evil spirits were ascending from the fiery pits of hell, but there is a much more scientific explanation. The geological makeup of the area surrounding the club is interesting, to say the least. In fact, it's downright strange and may lead us

Cracks from the fault line are shown in a retaining wall and in the parking lot. *Author's collection.*

to the ultimate truth about why the activity at Bobby Mackey's occurs at such high levels and is known as the "Holy Grail" by many paranormal investigators.

The findings of the geotechnical survey paint a strange picture of exactly what's happening below the ground at one of the world's most notorious paranormal hotspots. Underground running water was found. This can cause small fluctuations in electromagnetic disturbance.

While taking soil samples, it was found that even the soil lying on top of the ground had magnetic properties. Below the club lies a huge limestone deposit. Limestone has long been believed to play a role in paranormal events because of its ability to store information. If you find it hard to believe that rock could hold information, simply look to the technology of DVDs. A piece of plastic holds an entire movie with sound and video. It is believed that limestone can contribute to residual hauntings by storing and replaying information in an environment. In the same respect, it is unquestionably possible that a person's personality could be imprinted in a similar manner.

So then, are the spirits haunting Bobby Mackey's simply residual imprints from the past or intelligent beings? The answer is probably both. There have been many sightings of shadow figures by paranormal investigators.

Some reports have said that the sightings occur for several seconds, and if investigators call out to the shadow figures, they will not react or respond. It's as if the investigators are ghosts themselves. This seems to point to the possibility that at least some of the things happening around the club are residual in nature.

With the underground running water, magnetized soil and limestone deposit, a clear picture is beginning to emerge of just how important these factors may be in relation to the level of paranormal events occurring at the site. But even with all these findings, there was still something bigger happening under the club.

What the geotechnical survey found was that the club lies on a large fault line. This fault line is what was responsible for the earth opening up when Bobby was planning the new construction. It is also why the parking lot and basement are scarred with cracks, slopes and generally uneven properties.

When talking about fault lines, it is not uncommon to hear about something called the Tectonic Strain Theory. This theory was proposed by Michael Persinger in 1975. The theory states that geological formations on fault lines are put under immense pressure and generate extremely high electromagnetic fields. This theory says that some minerals do not produce electromagnetic fields by themselves, but when placed under the huge strain of a fault line, they can indeed create EM disturbances in their environment.

He suggested that during events of large EM release, glowing lights can be seen and may even explain UFO sightings. According to a study, more UFO sightings are reported during times of tectonic movement and strain that cause extremely high EM fields.

In this particular case, it's certainly possible that the electromagnetism generated during these shifts may be contributing to the paranormal events at Bobby Mackey's or at least contributing to the way people perceive them.

As part of Persinger's Tectonic Strain Theory, he proposed that exposure to the high EM fields produced near fault lines may cause hallucinations in the temporal lobe that relate to popular culture such as Bigfoot, ghosts or other extraordinary phenomena. Paranormal events are most definitely taking place at the location, and this theory can't explain away all of them. Is it possible, however, that some "paranormal" experiences that people report may be attributed to hallucinations caused by the EM disturbances? The answer is most certainly "yes" if you believe the theory to be true.

My personal belief is that the tectonic strain that is causing these sporadically high electromagnetic fields, the limestone deposit, the running water, the magnetic soil and all of their effects are causing a sort of perfect paranormal "storm" that maximizes the proper conditions needed for high-level paranormal events to occur. I've been speaking for years about the paranormal storm occurring beneath the haunted music club.

These elements working together can cause electromagnetic disturbances that some investigators perceive or interpret as the presence of a nonphysical spirit. I'm not suggesting that the geological factors discount all the experiences that people have had on the site, because those factors most certainly do not cause events such as voice phenomenon (VP), electronic voice phenomena (EVP) or physical interaction by ghosts. They might, however, raise a plausible scientific explanation for some or all of the extremely terrifying events that Carl Lawson experienced.

The site also produces regular ELF disturbances. ELF, known as extremely low frequencies, can cause a myriad of effects on the human body. ELF exposure has been suggested to cause skin redness, feelings of tingling and burning, headache, fatigue and nausea. All of these symptoms have been reported by paranormal investigators.

Another issue the fault line causes is geopathic stress. The term comes from the Greek words "geo," which means Earth, and "pathos," which means illness. An area with geopathic disturbances also affects the biological properties of living organisms. These disturbances can cause a wide variety of effects on humans who are exposed to the geomagnetic fluctuations. Those who are exposed for extended periods of time, such as Carl Lawson who lived in the upstairs apartment, can begin experiencing more extreme effects, such as auditory and visual hallucinations. The scientific properties present in a geopathic disturbance can also cause problems with pregnancy,

Management of the Latin Quarter installed a trapdoor over this staircase to elude arrest. Today it is the "staircase to nowhere." *Author's collection.*

such as miscarriage or premature labor. This would also be in line with some of the experiences women have had at the site.

Reports of paranormal phenomena are common at sites suffering geopathic stress. One property shared by geopathic stress and the manifestation of ghosts is the presence of gamma rays. Studies have shown that paranormal investigators may be exposing themselves to extremely dangerous radiation. A gamma ray is an electromagnetic energy photon. Gamma radiation is high-energy ionizing radiation. Gamma photons have no mass and no electric charge. They are pure electromagnetic energy. If you didn't follow the last few sentences, just understand that gamma rays are the most dangerous form of radiation known to man. They can pass through the body, leaving all of our internal organs exposed.

The site holds the correct conditions to also be host to telluric currents. Also known as "Earth currents," telluric currents describe electrical energy flowing on and below the Earth's surface. Telluric currents are used by geophysicists to map out structures beneath the Earth's surface, including fault lines. This electricity may either be fueling the paranormal activity at the haunted nightclub or somehow uncloaking the activity so it is more easily perceived.

With so many people reporting stories of ghosts following them home from Bobby Mackey's, is there any possible scientific explanation for how this is possible? Some people believe the scientific properties of the site are holding souls hostage, and the spirits are somehow trapped and unable to leave. How then do so many people experience strange things in their lives *after* visiting the location? Perhaps there *is* a scientific explanation.

For several years, I have been speaking at conferences and with those in the paranormal community about my theory to support the existence of a soul. I call it QUEST Theory. The acronym stands for "Quantum Unified Entangled Soul Theory."

First we must cover the topic of quantum entanglement. Sounds weird, huh? This physical phenomenon has been proven through scientific research. The phenomenon was shown to be present in the biological process of photosynthesis in plants. Effects having to do with quantum mechanics give green plants the ability to transfer solar energy from molecules into electrochemical reactions, nearly instantaneously. When quantum-sized particles become entangled, such as electrons, any change to one electron will instantly be shown in the other, no matter how great the distance between the two. The particles may be physically separated by space but act as a single system.

In the QUEST Theory, it is possible for two souls to become entangled on a quantum level, therefore affecting each other instantly. These shared changes could include any part of the human essence that survives after death, such as belief, habits and idiosyncrasies of personality. This theory may also explain how demonic possessions occur. After all, in a demonic possession, demons do not actually live inside a person's body. They overtake their free will. This could most certainly be done through quantum entanglement of a demon and a person.

We talked earlier about the role that emotion plays in the possibility of experiencing a spirit attachment. When the essence or soul of two individuals becomes entangled, one may be able to affect the other no matter the distance between them. If this is true, a person experiencing a spirit attachment could have very real physical, mental, emotional or spiritual events happen to them as a result of what is happening in the entangled soul of the spirit. This could also be how some "sensitives," including psychics and mediums, interpret information.

Possible scientific explanations are something to seriously consider in the case of this haunted nightclub. I have always said that if ghosts are manifesting to us, they must abide by the universal scientific laws of our world.

CHAPTER 15

REVELATIONS

The caretaker of the property today is Matt Coates. He has worked at the club since 2003, having various responsibilities such as head of security, maintenance and others. He has spent many hours in the club during operating hours as well as when the bar is closed. During these many hours of exposure, Coates said he has experienced encounters ranging from bizarre to terrifying.

When asked about what kinds of ghosts inhabit the country music club, he was quick to answer: "There are very dark spirits in this building." Coates said he has come in contact with the malevolent forces in the club on several occasions. During the filming of an episode of *Ghost Adventures*, Coates accompanied the investigators and says he was influenced by the dark spirits in the building. "I was borderline possessed," he said. Bishop James Long was forced to perform the Minor Rite of Exorcism on him to end the influence.

One Saturday morning in the dead of winter, Coates was alone working in the basement to replace a frozen pipe. Standing just outside the room of faces, Coates said he heard something out of the ordinary. He stood still in order to discern what the sound was. "All of the sudden," he said, "something grabbed me under my arms and picked me up about a foot off the ground!" He said the entity then physically threw him several feet across the room. "I wasn't hallucinating, and I didn't trip," he explained.

Coates says aside from the extreme physical attack that he experienced in the basement, he has experienced many other instances of spirit manifestations throughout the building. "I've seen what appears to be the silhouette of a woman without a head in here," he said. "I've seen another woman in a white dress. I've even chased a big black dog through here until it vanished into thin air." Coates explained that sometimes the apparitions appear solid like a person, and at other times they can be transparent. Many times, he says, it is simply catching a glimpse of something in your peripheral vision. "Sometimes I can't say 100 percent that I've seen a ghost," said Coates. "I see stuff out of the corner of my eye."

He admits that he has no idea why he would see a headless woman, knowing full well that there is no connection of the Pearl Bryan murder to the site. "I don't know," he said. "Sometimes I wonder if we're imagining what we're seeing with all the stories that have been told." He said that there have been many times when his experiences have nearly scared him away permanently. "There have been so many times that I've thrown my keys at Bobby and said, 'I'm done and I'm never coming back,'" he said. "Then I'm back the next day because something keeps drawing me back."

Coates believes that the bizarre properties occurring at the site may be playing a role in what people are experiencing. "Because of the properties of the land, people are thinking in their minds that this certain ghost is supposed to be here," he suggested. It is most certainly possible that the power of suggestion may be influencing some of those who visit the location. People that spend a lot of time there are the ones reporting high-level experiences. Is it that they are just there more often than others and have a greater chance of witnessing something incredible? Or could it be that they are being affected by long-term exposure to the scientific properties of the site?

When I asked Coates if he believes the haunting will ever be resolved or come to an end, he replied, "I think they'll always be here." What advice, I asked him, would he give to those visiting the club? "Don't come in here provoking. You get to go home, then I have to deal with the fallout." He said he can tell a difference in the environment after someone comes in with a disrespectful attitude. "I can feel the energy change after someone provokes. I don't know how to describe it. It just doesn't feel right."

We have explored the long history of tragedy that has occurred on the site of Bobby Mackey's Music World and has laid the foundation for one of the world's most extreme paranormal locations. We have gone deep inside the terrifying experiences that many people have reported, including a demonic possession and exorcism. We have also examined the geotechnical properties of the site and possible scientific explanations for the extreme paranormal activity at the nightclub.

It seems that the tragic events that have taken place on or near the property may play a key role in the paranormal claims that continue to pour out of the site. Disembodied souls haunt properties for many reasons, such as guilt, fear of judgment or even to take revenge on the living.

The things people experience at the country music bar are on a high level when looking at paranormal activity in general. Bobby Mackey continues to stand firm in his assertion that he doesn't believe in ghosts, although he has admitted he doesn't like being alone inside the club. "I don't understand how that's possible," Bobby told me. His view is that perhaps he just doesn't have the ability to sense spirits. Some people are naturally good at singing, artwork or other talents, he says. Bobby believes that some people may be naturally better at perceiving ghosts. When I asked him how he feels about the hundreds of stories people tell about their experiences, he answered simply, "Maybe they can perceive something I can't."

In the end, Bobby's one true love is country music. And he does it better than anybody in the greater Cincinnati area. For him, owning a haunted nightclub does not explain who he is as a person. Nevertheless, the paranormal aspect of the club attracts thousands of visitors every year, hoping to get a glimpse of the ghosts that so hopelessly roam the building.

When Carl Lawson began sharing his story with others, he faced ridicule and harsh judgment. Even believers find his stories hard to swallow. There is no doubt in my mind that what Carl experienced was extremely real to him. During the chats I had with him over the years, the toll of what he experienced was written all over his face as he recalled events. Carl passed away on January 26, 2012, leaving behind a legacy of terror and triumph.

The many events that Carl reported have led some to suggest that he might have been suffering from schizophrenia. The reports of electricity rushing through the body, as well as auditory and visual hallucinations, can occur in people affected by this disease. In the spirit of covering all possible explanations, it is surely a possibility. On the other hand, medical science does not yet have an explanation for schizophrenia and knows very little about the disease. Some people believe that the symptoms of schizophrenia might actually be a demonic possession, or vice versa. A study of those with schizophrenia found that 24 percent of patients had religious delusions.

Was Carl experiencing the symptoms of a mental disease? Was he influenced by the strange scientific properties the site holds? Even if what Carl experienced were merely hallucinations, it does not explain the many encounters that others have reported. While we may never fully understand what Carl experienced, to him it was as real as anything in life. No matter what the correct explanation may be, Carl was a tortured soul who endured terrifying experiences. He was a simple man and wanted nothing more than

A view of the stage inside the "Most Haunted Nightclub in America." *Author's collection.*

peace following the exorcism. He found that peace, although he once told me, "They're always around me. I feel them." He was well aware that he had defeated his demons and thanked God every day for it.

In all of my efforts, and with the help of private investigators, I was unable to find any documentation about Johana Jewell or her lover Robert Randall. The few possibilities simply did not match up according to time or ties to the area. But people definitely smell ghostly rose perfume throughout the building, and it is said to be a sign that Johana is around. One thing I have learned in my experience with the haunted nightclub is that the spirits there will portray themselves as whoever you want them to be in order to open a line of communication. Human spirits or demons, the ghosts find amusement in affecting the living.

Whether you find yourself as a visitor of the nightclub enjoying Bobby Mackey's unique brand of country music or investigating the property looking for ghosts, keep one thing in mind: you're never really alone.

Time has bruised and battered the site with betrayal, deception, lies and death. The club forges ahead today with entertainment, friends, happiness and life. Armed with the truth and many possible explanations, it's now up to you to decide why this location's unrested souls have made it the "Most Haunted Nightclub in America."

BIBLIOGRAPHY

Ancestry.com. "Earnest P Brady." Accessed May 31, 2013.

Billboard. "Newport, Ky., LQ Sold for $100,000." July 24, 1948.

———. "Two Ky. Clubs Do a Fold Up." January 26, 1952.

Breaux, Brenda. "Crack in the Earth Breaking this Ol' Country Boy's Heart." *Cincinnati Enquirer*, July 15, 1993.

Carr, Mike. Interview with the author. May 14, 2013.

Cincinnati Enquirer. "Primrose May Be Padlocked as Result of Fatal Fist Fight." November 21, 1943.

———. "Sailor Dies at Hospital—Son of Primrose Owner." December 13, 1944.

Cincinnati Times-Star. "Found Skull Hidden." August 18, 1902.

———. "Hectic Career of George Remus Ends." January 21, 1952.

———. "Obituary of E.P. Brady." December 12, 1944.

Coates, Matt. Interview with the author. July 26, 2013.

Dedman, Chris. Interview with the author. June 12, 2013.

Deed Book 10. Newport, KY: Campbell County Property Valuation Administrator. 15, 16, 22, 24, 336, 425.

Deed Book 105. Newport, KY: Campbell County Property Valuation Administrator. 260, 271.

Deed Book 107. Newport, KY: Campbell County Property Valuation Administrator. 531.

Deed Book 110. Newport, KY: Campbell County Property Valuation Administrator. 265.

Deed Book 118. Newport, KY: Campbell County Property Valuation Administrator. 253.

Deed Book 12. Newport, KY: Campbell County Property Valuation Administrator. 627.

Deed Book 126. Newport, KY: Campbell County Property Valuation Administrator. 355.

Deed Book 134. Newport, KY: Campbell County Property Valuation Administrator. 448.

Deed Book 143. Newport, KY: Campbell County Property Valuation Administrator. 123.

Deed Book 15. Newport, KY: Campbell County Property Valuation Administrator. 346, 393.

Deed Book 168. Newport, KY: Campbell County Property Valuation Administrator. 201, 202.

Deed Book 174. Newport, KY: Campbell County Property Valuation Administrator. 557.

Deed Book 177. Newport, KY: Campbell County Property Valuation Administrator. 415.

Deed Book 187. Newport, KY: Campbell County Property Valuation Administrator. 399.

Deed Book 195. Newport, KY: Campbell County Property Valuation Administrator. 213.

Deed Book 212. Newport, KY: Campbell County Property Valuation Administrator. 480.

Deed Book 213. Newport, KY: Campbell County Property Valuation Administrator. 168.

Deed Book 222. Newport, KY: Campbell County Property Valuation Administrator. 331.

Deed Book 223. Newport, KY: Campbell County Property Valuation Administrator. 275.

Deed Book 228. Newport, KY: Campbell County Property Valuation Administrator. 11, 211.

Deed Book 262. Newport, KY: Campbell County Property Valuation Administrator. 447.

Deed Book 291. Newport, KY: Campbell County Property Valuation Administrator. 514.

Deed Book 30. Newport, KY: Campbell County Property Valuation Administrator. 106.

Deed Book 462. Newport, KY: Campbell County Property Valuation Administrator. 26, 31.

Deed Book 56. Newport, KY: Campbell County Property Valuation Administrator. 27.

Deed Book 60. Newport, KY: Campbell County Property Valuation Administrator. 266.

Deed Book 72. Newport, KY: Campbell County Property Valuation Administrator. 208.

Deed Book 75. Newport, KY: Campbell County Property Valuation Administrator. 20, 164.

Deed Book 79. Newport, KY: Campbell County Property Valuation Administrator. 20.

Deed Book 8. Newport, KY: Campbell County Property Valuation Administrator. 146.

Encyclopedia Britannica. "Telluric Current." Accessed July 14, 2013. http://www.britannica.com/EBchecked/topic/586372/telluric-current.

Gavin, Tim. Interview with the author. May 27, 2013.

General James Taylor Family Papers. Eva G. Farris Special Collections. Steely Library, Northern Kentucky University.

"Geopathic Stress: Harmful Energies from the Earth." Accessed July 14, 2013. http://www.geopathology.com/geopathic-stress.html.

Geraldo Riviera Show. "A Real Life Exorcism." *YouTube video,* 37:58, October 30, 1992. http://www.youtube.com/watch?v=jBCJ6z30Zls.

Ghost Adventures. "Bobby Mackey's Music World." Directed by Zak Bagans. My Tupelo Entertainment, October 17, 2008.

Ghost Adventures. "Return to Bobby Mackey's." Directed by Zak Bagans. My Tupelo Entertainment, October 1, 2010.

Greene, Brian. *The Elegant Universe: Superstrings, Hidden Dimensions, and the Quest for the Ultimate Theory.* New York: Maple-Vail Book Manufacturing Group, 2003.

Hamblin, Dale. Interview with the author. July 11, 2013.

Kentucky Journal. "More Indictments." June 13, 1893.

Kentucky New Era. "Gambling Syndicate Acquires New Club." March 11, 1949. http://news.google.com/newspapers?nid=266&dat=19490310&id=AfArAAAAIBAJ&sjid=Z2cFAAAAIBAJ&pg=5770,2404876 (accessed July 13, 2013).

———. "Pearl Bryan's Head Found." March 21, 1896. http://news.google.com/newspapers?nid=266&dat=18960321&id=vHM0AAAAIBAJ&sjid=IrIFAAAAIBAJ&pg=3574,677460 (accessed May 2, 2013).

Kentucky Post. "Accident Fatal to John Beiting." July 28, 1933.

———. "Brady Back at Pen—Covington Bootlegger Surrenders After 26 Day Vacation." March 1, 1925.

———. "Brady Freed by Jury." December 21, 1926.

———. "Brady on Bond." April 9, 1923.

———. "Brady to Assist Detective in Liquor Death." July 26, 1928.

———. "Brady to Fight for his Life." December 18, 1926.

———. "Brady Trial Disappoints Spectators." July 3, 1930.

———. "Buck Brady on Trial." April 6, 1923.

———. "Burglar Gets Break as Gun Fails to Fire." September 4, 1931.

———. "Cafe is Robbed." November 11, 1941.

———. "Campbell-Co. Grand Jury [Has] Furnished Names of Gambling Houses and Places Where Slot Machines Were Operating." June 27, 1929.

———. "Cocaine Found!" February 12, 1896.

———. "Don't Stop with Brady's Place Mr. Fuller." July 1, 1930.

———. "Firemen Busy Over Holiday." November 28, 1930.

———. "Guilty Verdict for Brady." April 7, 1923.

———. "Head Cut Off!" February 1, 1896.

———. "Held in Detroit." February 28, 1930.

———. "History of the Ft. Thomas Murder." April 7, 1896.

———. "Lawrence Howard Is Shot." October 19, 1926.

———. "Licking Pike Cafe Burned: Loss is $4,000." March 1, 1937.

———. "The Merciless Ax of Time." November 2, 1915. http://nkyviews. com/campbell/text/newport_hanging_tree.htm (accessed June 2, 2013).

———. "Newport Gambling Den Closed." June 28, 1930.

———. "Pearl Bryan's Skull Found in Newport?" February 18, 1907.

———. "Pearl Bryan Was Decapitated, Says the Coroner's Jury." February 12, 1896.

———. "Popp's Place Visited." November 29, 1922.

———. "Prison Looms." April 23, 1923.

———. "Probe Goes On as Life Ebbs." October 20, 1926.

———. "Public Fooled in Disposal of Scott Jackson's Body." March 20, 1922.

———. "Rush Trial of Buck Brady." October 26, 1922.

———. "Skull That May Have Been Pearl Bryan's." September 27, 1897.

———. "Slaying Story Told in Court." December 20, 1926.

———. "Sues Partner in Night Club; Asks Receiver." September 7, 1940.

———. "Testimony of Experts Offered by the Defense Against Similar Testimony of the Prosecution." May 1, 1896.

———. "Three Taken in U.S. Raids." April 20, 1920.

———. "To the Grave." March 27, 1896.

———. "Troops to Stay." March 16, 1922.

———. "What Does This Mean?" July 3, 1930.

———. "Whisky Thefts Are Probed." April 5, 1920.

———. "A Wild Steer." May 3, 1892.

———. "Wounds Fatal to Howard." October 21, 1926.

———. "You Didn't Mess with Buck." February 10, 2003.

Kentucky State Journal. "The City." September 11, 1880.

———. "Explosion and Fire—$1,200 Damage." September 6, 1888.

———. "Explosion at [Robson's] Distillery." September 6, 1888.

Kentucky Times Star. "Campbell County Jury Backs Up State Police." February 16, 1955.

———. "Check Up Made at Distillery." June 2, 1922.

———. "Company Will Pay Expense—Ten-Inch Water Main to be Laid." November 12, 1913.

———. "Distillery Has Changed Hands—Jacob Speyer." September 10, 1920.

———. "Employees of Distillery Arraigned." June 1, 1922.

———. "Federal Seizure." February 20, 1923.

———. "Fight Fire in Building Adjoining Distillery." January 29, 1914.

———. "Fine of $500 and Costs for Earnest Brady." July 8, 1920.

———. "Head of Old 76 Distillery Placed on Trial." December 5, 1922.

———. "9 Employees of Wilder Casino Held—Patrons Fined $50 Plus Costs." January 4, 1955.

———. "Structures of Old 76 Are Purchased." June 25, 1920.

———. "Woman Testified That She Drank High Balls." July 7, 1920.

Lawson, Carl. Interview with the author. October 31, 2010.

———. *Transcription of "Johana Jewell" Journal Found by Carl Lawson.* Unpublished, 2011.

Long, Bishop James. Interview with the author. May 30, 2013.

Mackey, Bobby. Interview with the author. May 01, 2013.

Master Commissioner Deed Book 3. Newport, KY: Campbell County Property Valuation Administrator. 219.

Master Commissioner Deed Book 9. Newport, KY: Campbell County Property Valuation Administrator. 329.

Northern Kentucky Views. "Licking Bridge Collapse." Accessed July 9, 2013. http://www.nkyviews.com/kenton/text/kenton_text_licking_bridge.htm.

Roemer, Jeff. Interview with the author. June 06, 2013.

ScienceDaily. "Untangling the Quantum Entanglement Behind Photosynthesis." http://www.sciencedaily.com/releases/2010/05/100510151356.htm (accessed July 14, 2013).

Siddle, R., G. Haddock, N. Tarrier and E.B. Faragher. *"Religious Delusions in*

Patients Admitted to the Hospital with Schizophrenia." Unpublished manuscript, 2002. http://www.ncbi.nlm.nih.gov/pubmed/11990010.

Speigel, Lee. "Spooky Number of Americans Believe in Ghosts." *Huffington Post*, February 2, 2013. http://www.huffingtonpost.com/2013/02/02/real-ghosts-americans-poll_n_2049485.html. Accessed June 14, 2013.

Ticket. "New Distillery is Nearing Completion in Finchtown." June 17, 1875.

United States Court of Appeals, Sixth Circuit. *United States of America, Plaintiff-Appellee v. George Serian Gebhart, David Fleming Whitfield, Harold Cordell Smith, Defendants-Appellants.* Last modified May 07, 1971. Accessed June 3, 2013. https://bulk.resource.org/courts.gov/c/F2/441/441.F2d.1261.20425-20427.html.

United States Senate. "Investigation of organized crime in interstate commerce. Hearings before a Special Committee to Investigate Organized Crime in Interstate Commerce, United States Senate, Eighty-first Congress, Second Session, pursuant to S. Res. 202." Accessed July 13, 2013. http://www.archive.org/stream/investigationofo15unit/investigationofo15unit_djvu.txt.

Velasquez, Rick. Interview with the author. June 2, 2013.

Will Book 12. Newport, KY: Campbell County Property Valuation Administrator. 565.

Wilson, Becca. Interview with the author. July 14, 2013.

ABOUT THE AUTHOR

Dan lives in Cincinnati, Ohio, where he is owner/operator of Haunted Cincinnati Tours. He is founder of C.A.U.G.H.T. ParaScience, a paranormal research and development team that develops new technology for the field of paranormal studies. In his spare time, Dan enjoys uncovering the lost stories of local history. He works today to legitimize the paranormal field by passing on his knowledge, passion and respect of the paranormal world to others. Through lectures, field studies and assisting families, Dan works as an advocate for those who have experienced extreme paranormal encounters.

Visit us at
www.historypress.net
···
This title is also available as an e-book